TEACHER'S PET PUBLICATIONS

PUZZLE PACK
for
Hatchet

based on the book by
Gary Paulsen

Written by
William T. Collins

© 2005 Teacher's Pet Publications
All Rights Reserved

The materials in this packet are copyrighted
by Teacher's Pet Publications, Inc.

These pages may be duplicated by the purchaser
for use in the purchaser's own classroom.

Copying any of these materials and distributing them
for any other purpose is a violation of the copyright laws.

© 2005 Teacher's Pet Publications, Inc.
www.tpet.com

INTRODUCTION
If you already own the LitPlan for this title, this Puzzle Pack will refresh your Unit Resource Materials and Vocabulary Resource Materials sections plus give you additional materials you can substitute into the tests. If you do not already have a complete LitPlan, these pages will give you some supplemental materials to use with your own plan. There are two main groups of materials: one set for unit words (such as characters' names, symbols, places, etc.) and one set for vocabulary words associated with the book.

WORD LIST
There is a word list for both the unit words and the vocabulary words. These lists show you which words are being used in the materials and the clues or definitions being used for those words. You may want to give students a word list with clues/definitions to help them, or you may want students to only have a word list (without clues/definitions) if you want them to work a little harder. Both are available for duplication. The word lists can also be your "calling key" for the bingo games.

FILL IN THE BLANK AND MATCHING
There are 4 each of the fill in the blank and matching worksheets for both the unit and vocabulary words. These pages can be used either as extra worksheets for students or as objective parts of a unit test. They can be done individually if students need extra help or as a whole class activity to review the material covered.

MAGIC SQUARES
The magic squares not only reinforce the material covered but also work on reasoning and math skills. Many teachers have told us that their students really enjoy doing these!

WORD SEARCH PUZZLES
The word search words go in all directions, as indicated on your answer keys. Two of the word search puzzles have the clues listed rather than the words. This makes the puzzle a little more difficult, but it reinforces the material better. Two word search puzzles have words only for students who find the clue puzzles too difficult.

CROSSWORD PUZZLES
Both unit and vocabulary word sections have 4 crossword puzzles.

BINGO CARDS
There are 32 individual bingo cards for the unit words and 32 individual bingo cards for the vocabulary words. You can use your word list as a "call list," calling the words at random and marking them off of your list as you go, or you could use the flash cards by cutting them apart and drawing the words at random from a hat (or box or whatever). To make a better review, you might ask for the definition and spelling of each word as you call it out–or you could call out the definitions and have students tell you the words they need to look for on the puzzle.

JUGGLE LETTERS
The vocabulary juggle letter game is intended to help students learn the spellings of the words. One sheet has the definitions listed on it as an extra help for students who need it or to reinforce the definitions if you choose to do so.

FLASH CARDS
We've included a set of vocabulary flash cards you can duplicate, cut, and fold for your students. Some teachers make a few sets for general use by the class; others make a set for each student. Some teachers duplicate them for each student and have the students cut & fold their own. You can cut out just the words and put them in a hat, have each student pick out one word and write the definition and a sentence for that word. Students then swap words and papers, with the next student adding a sentence of his own under the last one. You can have students swap as many times as you like. Each time the student will read the sentences written prior to his own and then add a sentence. You can cut out the words and definitions separately and play "I Have; Who Has?" Each student in the room draws a word and definition. The first student says, "I have (the name of the word). Who has the definition?" The student with the definition reads it then says, "I have (the name of the vocabulary word she has). Who has the definition?" The round continues until all words and definitions have been given.

Hatchet Word List

No.	Word	Clue/Definition
1.	AMBER	Mall where Brian saw his mother and the other man
2.	BEAR	It saw Brian near the berry bushes but did not attack
3.	BOW	Brian used a ___ and arrows to kill the rabbits
4.	BRIAN	Teenage wilderness survivor
5.	BRUSHPILE	Raft Brian built to get to the plane: ___ One
6.	CANADA	Where Brian was going
7.	CESSNA	Model of the plane that crashed
8.	CHERRIES	Brian's first food
9.	DIVORCE	What Brian's parents had gotten
10.	DREAMS	They helped Brian think of ways to survive
11.	FIFTYFOUR	Number of days Brian spent in the wilderness
12.	FIRE	Friend that Brian created
13.	FLOATS	The plane that rescued Brian had these
14.	FOOLBIRD	First Meat
15.	FUR	The ___ buyer rescued Brian
16.	HATCHET	Gift from Brian's mother
17.	HUNGER	It drove Brian to hunt
18.	LAKE	Plane crashed into it
19.	LEDGE	Where Brian stored his food after the skunk got the eggs
20.	MOOSE	The senseless attack of this animal drove Brian into the water
21.	MOSQUITOES	They made a living coat on Brian's skin
22.	PAULSEN	Author
23.	PERPICH	Teacher who told students to value themselves
24.	PILOT	He died of a heart attack
25.	POND	Brian built one to store the fresh fish
26.	PORCUPINE	Attack of this animal caused Brian to create fire
27.	PRESS	Interested in Brian for a few months upon his return
28.	RASPBERRIES	Brian's second food
29.	ROBESON	Mr. ___ worked in the oil fields in Canada
30.	SEARCH	The ___ plane didn't see Brian and turned away
31.	SECRET	The ___ was that Brian saw his mother with another man
32.	SURVIVAL	Brian got the ___ pack from the back of the plane
33.	TERRY	Pretended to be lost in the woods with Brian
34.	THIRTEEN	Brian's age
35.	TORNADO	It destroyed Brian's shelter
36.	TOUGH	That Brian knew he could learn and survive was ___ Hope
37.	TRANSMITTER	Brian unknowingly activated the emergency one
38.	TURTLE	Brian took its eggs for food
39.	TWO	Number of hours Brian was blinded by the skunk
40.	YORK	Plane started out in New ___

Hatchet Fill In The Blank 1

_____ 1. Plane crashed into it
_____ 2. They helped Brian think of ways to survive
_____ 3. The senseless attack of this animal drove Brian into the water
_____ 4. That Brian knew he could learn and survive was ___ Hope
_____ 5. Mr. ___ worked in the oil fields in Canada
_____ 6. He died of a heart attack
_____ 7. Interested in Brian for a few months upon his return
_____ 8. It saw Brian near the berry bushes but did not attack
_____ 9. Brian's age
_____ 10. Brian's second food
_____ 11. Number of hours Brian was blinded by the skunk
_____ 12. Gift from Brian's mother
_____ 13. Where Brian stored his food after the skunk got the eggs
_____ 14. The ___ was that Brian saw his mother with another man
_____ 15. Brian got the ___ pack from the back of the plane
_____ 16. Brian took its eggs for food
_____ 17. The ___ plane didn't see Brian and turned away
_____ 18. Teacher who told students to value themselves
_____ 19. They made a living coat on Brian's skin
_____ 20. Author

Hatchet Fill In The Blank 1 Answer Key

LAKE	1. Plane crashed into it
DREAMS	2. They helped Brian think of ways to survive
MOOSE	3. The senseless attack of this animal drove Brian into the water
TOUGH	4. That Brian knew he could learn and survive was ___ Hope
ROBESON	5. Mr. ___ worked in the oil fields in Canada
PILOT	6. He died of a heart attack
PRESS	7. Interested in Brian for a few months upon his return
BEAR	8. It saw Brian near the berry bushes but did not attack
THIRTEEN	9. Brian's age
RASPBERRIES	10. Brian's second food
TWO	11. Number of hours Brian was blinded by the skunk
HATCHET	12. Gift from Brian's mother
LEDGE	13. Where Brian stored his food after the skunk got the eggs
SECRET	14. The ___ was that Brian saw his mother with another man
SURVIVAL	15. Brian got the ___ pack from the back of the plane
TURTLE	16. Brian took its eggs for food
SEARCH	17. The ___ plane didn't see Brian and turned away
PERPICH	18. Teacher who told students to value themselves
MOSQUITOES	19. They made a living coat on Brian's skin
PAULSEN	20. Author

Copyrighted

Hatchet Fill In The Blank 2

_____

_____

_____

_____

_____

_____

_____

_____

_____

_____

_____

_____

_____

_____

_____

_____

_____

_____

_____

_____

1. The senseless attack of this animal drove Brian into the water
2. Plane started out in New ___
3. Brian's second food
4. Gift from Brian's mother
5. Plane crashed into it
6. Brian used a ___ and arrows to kill the rabbits
7. Pretended to be lost in the woods with Brian
8. Teacher who told students to value themselves
9. Where Brian stored his food after the skunk got the eggs
10. The ___ plane didn't see Brian and turned away
11. Brian unknowingly activated the emergency one
12. It drove Brian to hunt
13. Model of the plane that crashed
14. Author
15. Where Brian was going
16. Brian's first food
17. Interested in Brian for a few months upon his return
18. Brian got the ___ pack from the back of the plane
19. Raft Brian built to get to the plane: ___ One
20. That Brian knew he could learn and survive was ___ Hope

Hatchet Fil In The Blank 2 Answer Key

Answer	Clue
MOOSE	1. The senseless attack of this animal drove Brian into the water
YORK	2. Plane started out in New ___
RASPBERRIES	3. Brian's second food
HATCHET	4. Gift from Brian's mother
LAKE	5. Plane crashed into it
BOW	6. Brian used a ___ and arrows to kill the rabbits
TERRY	7. Pretended to be lost in the woods with Brian
PERPICH	8. Teacher who told students to value themselves
LEDGE	9. Where Brian stored his food after the skunk got the eggs
SEARCH	10. The ___ plane didn't see Brian and turned away
TRANSMITTER	11. Brian unknowingly activated the emergency one
HUNGER	12. It drove Brian to hunt
CESSNA	13. Model of the plane that crashed
PAULSEN	14. Author
CANADA	15. Where Brian was going
CHERRIES	16. Brian's first food
PRESS	17. Interested in Brian for a few months upon his return
SURVIVAL	18. Brian got the ___ pack from the back of the plane
BRUSHPILE	19. Raft Brian built to get to the plane: ___ One
TOUGH	20. That Brian knew he could learn and survive was ___ Hope

Hatchet Fill In The Blank 3

_____ 1. What Brian's parents had gotten
_____ 2. Brian took its eggs for food
_____ 3. Interested in Brian for a few months upon his return
_____ 4. They helped Brian think of ways to survive
_____ 5. Mall where Brian saw his mother and the other man
_____ 6. The ___ buyer rescued Brian
_____ 7. Brian used a ___ and arrows to kill the rabbits
_____ 8. The ___ plane didn't see Brian and turned away
_____ 9. Teenage wilderness survivor
_____ 10. The ___ was that Brian saw his mother with another man
_____ 11. It drove Brian to hunt
_____ 12. That Brian knew he could learn and survive was ___ Hope
_____ 13. Brian's first food
_____ 14. Number of hours Brian was blinded by the skunk
_____ 15. Pretended to be lost in the woods with Brian
_____ 16. Model of the plane that crashed
_____ 17. It destroyed Brian's shelter
_____ 18. It saw Brian near the berry bushes but did not attack
_____ 19. Gift from Brian's mother
_____ 20. He died of a heart attack

Hatchet Fill In The Blank 3 Answer Key

DIVORCE	1. What Brian's parents had gotten
TURTLE	2. Brian took its eggs for food
PRESS	3. Interested in Brian for a few months upon his return
DREAMS	4. They helped Brian think of ways to survive
AMBER	5. Mall where Brian saw his mother and the other man
FUR	6. The ___ buyer rescued Brian
BOW	7. Brian used a ___ and arrows to kill the rabbits
SEARCH	8. The ___ plane didn't see Brian and turned away
BRIAN	9. Teenage wilderness survivor
SECRET	10. The ___ was that Brian saw his mother with another man
HUNGER	11. It drove Brian to hunt
TOUGH	12. That Brian knew he could learn and survive was ___ Hope
CHERRIES	13. Brian's first food
TWO	14. Number of hours Brian was blinded by the skunk
TERRY	15. Pretended to be lost in the woods with Brian
CESSNA	16. Model of the plane that crashed
TORNADO	17. It destroyed Brian's shelter
BEAR	18. It saw Brian near the berry bushes but did not attack
HATCHET	19. Gift from Brian's mother
PILOT	20. He died of a heart attack

Hatchet Fill In The Blank 4

_____   1. Number of hours Brian was blinded by the skunk
_____   2. Brian built one to store the fresh fish
_____   3. The senseless attack of this animal drove Brian into the water
_____   4. Teacher who told students to value themselves
_____   5. It destroyed Brian's shelter
_____   6. Author
_____   7. Brian unknowingly activated the emergency one
_____   8. Brian's first food
_____   9. Interested in Brian for a few months upon his return
_____   10. It drove Brian to hunt
_____   11. First Meat
_____   12. What Brian's parents had gotten
_____   13. Where Brian stored his food after the skunk got the eggs
_____   14. Where Brian was going
_____   15. Gift from Brian's mother
_____   16. The ___ plane didn't see Brian and turned away
_____   17. Plane started out in New ___
_____   18. Brian's second food
_____   19. The plane that rescued Brian had these
_____   20. They made a living coat on Brian's skin

Hatchet Fill In The Blank 4 Answer Key

Answer	Clue
TWO	1. Number of hours Brian was blinded by the skunk
POND	2. Brian built one to store the fresh fish
MOOSE	3. The senseless attack of this animal drove Brian into the water
PERPICH	4. Teacher who told students to value themselves
TORNADO	5. It destroyed Brian's shelter
PAULSEN	6. Author
TRANSMITTER	7. Brian unknowingly activated the emergency one
CHERRIES	8. Brian's first food
PRESS	9. Interested in Brian for a few months upon his return
HUNGER	10. It drove Brian to hunt
FOOLBIRD	11. First Meat
DIVORCE	12. What Brian's parents had gotten
LEDGE	13. Where Brian stored his food after the skunk got the eggs
CANADA	14. Where Brian was going
HATCHET	15. Gift from Brian's mother
SEARCH	16. The ___ plane didn't see Brian and turned away
YORK	17. Plane started out in New ___
RASPBERRIES	18. Brian's second food
FLOATS	19. The plane that rescued Brian had these
MOSQUITOES	20. They made a living coat on Brian's skin

Hatchet Matching 1

___ 1. CANADA   A. The ___ buyer rescued Brian
___ 2. BRIAN   B. Number of days Brian spent in the wilderness
___ 3. PORCUPINE   C. The senseless attack of this animal drove Brian into the water
___ 4. SURVIVAL   D. Plane crashed into it
___ 5. POND   E. Brian used a ___ and arrows to kill the rabbits
___ 6. RASPBERRIES   F. It drove Brian to hunt
___ 7. ROBESON   G. Brian's second food
___ 8. HUNGER   H. They helped Brian think of ways to survive
___ 9. FIFTYFOUR   I. Brian's age
___10. PERPICH   J. Brian unknowingly activated the emergency one
___11. BOW   K. Brian built one to store the fresh fish
___12. PRESS   L. Attack of this animal caused Brian to create fire
___13. MOOSE   M. They made a living coat on Brian's skin
___14. TERRY   N. Number of hours Brian was blinded by the skunk
___15. FOOLBIRD   O. Mr. ___ worked in the oil fields in Canada
___16. THIRTEEN   P. Interested in Brian for a few months upon his return
___17. CESSNA   Q. Brian got the ___ pack from the back of the plane
___18. LAKE   R. Brian's first food
___19. FUR   S. Model of the plane that crashed
___20. DREAMS   T. Where Brian was going
___21. MOSQUITOES   U. Teacher who told students to value themselves
___22. LEDGE   V. Teenage wilderness survivor
___23. CHERRIES   W. Pretended to be lost in the woods with Brian
___24. TRANSMITTER   X. Where Brian stored his food after the skunk got the eggs
___25. TWO   Y. First Meat

Hatchet Matching 1 Answer Key

T - 1. CANADA	A.	The ___ buyer rescued Brian
V - 2. BRIAN	B.	Number of days Brian spent in the wilderness
L - 3. PORCUPINE	C.	The senseless attack of this animal drove Brian into the water
Q - 4. SURVIVAL	D.	Plane crashed into it
K - 5. POND	E.	Brian used a ___ and arrows to kill the rabbits
G - 6. RASPBERRIES	F.	It drove Brian to hunt
O - 7. ROBESON	G.	Brian's second food
F - 8. HUNGER	H.	They helped Brian think of ways to survive
B - 9. FIFTYFOUR	I.	Brian's age
U - 10. PERPICH	J.	Brian unknowingly activated the emergency one
E - 11. BOW	K.	Brian built one to store the fresh fish
P - 12. PRESS	L.	Attack of this animal caused Brian to create fire
C - 13. MOOSE	M.	They made a living coat on Brian's skin
W - 14. TERRY	N.	Number of hours Brian was blinded by the skunk
Y - 15. FOOLBIRD	O.	Mr. ___ worked in the oil fields in Canada
I - 16. THIRTEEN	P.	Interested in Brian for a few months upon his return
S - 17. CESSNA	Q.	Brian got the ___ pack from the back of the plane
D - 18. LAKE	R.	Brian's first food
A - 19. FUR	S.	Model of the plane that crashed
H - 20. DREAMS	T.	Where Brian was going
M - 21. MOSQUITOES	U.	Teacher who told students to value themselves
X - 22. LEDGE	V.	Teenage wilderness survivor
R - 23. CHERRIES	W.	Pretended to be lost in the woods with Brian
J - 24. TRANSMITTER	X.	Where Brian stored his food after the skunk got the eggs
N - 25. TWO	Y.	First Meat

Hatchet Matching 2

___ 1. TRANSMITTER   A. Brian's second food

___ 2. DIVORCE   B. Mall where Brian saw his mother and the other man

___ 3. SEARCH   C. That Brian knew he could learn and survive was ___ Hope

___ 4. FUR   D. The plane that rescued Brian had these

___ 5. BOW   E. They made a living coat on Brian's skin

___ 6. PORCUPINE   F. It saw Brian near the berry bushes but did not attack

___ 7. ROBESON   G. What Brian's parents had gotten

___ 8. RASPBERRIES   H. Brian's age

___ 9. DREAMS   I. Brian built one to store the fresh fish

___10. TORNADO   J. Plane crashed into it

___11. LAKE   K. They helped Brian think of ways to survive

___12. BEAR   L. Brian unknowingly activated the emergency one

___13. FLOATS   M. Brian got the ___ pack from the back of the plane

___14. MOSQUITOES   N. The senseless attack of this animal drove Brian into the water

___15. HUNGER   O. Brian used a ___ and arrows to kill the rabbits

___16. AMBER   P. Teenage wilderness survivor

___17. TERRY   Q. It drove Brian to hunt

___18. MOOSE   R. First Meat

___19. SURVIVAL   S. Model of the plane that crashed

___20. BRIAN   T. The ___ buyer rescued Brian

___21. POND   U. The ___ plane didn't see Brian and turned away

___22. CESSNA   V. Pretended to be lost in the woods with Brian

___23. TOUGH   W. Mr. ___ worked in the oil fields in Canada

___24. FOOLBIRD   X. Attack of this animal caused Brian to create fire

___25. THIRTEEN   Y. It destroyed Brian's shelter

Hatchet Matching 2 Answer Key

L - 1. TRANSMITTER	A.	Brian's second food
G - 2. DIVORCE	B.	Mall where Brian saw his mother and the other man
U - 3. SEARCH	C.	That Brian knew he could learn and survive was ___ Hope
T - 4. FUR	D.	The plane that rescued Brian had these
O - 5. BOW	E.	They made a living coat on Brian's skin
X - 6. PORCUPINE	F.	It saw Brian near the berry bushes but did not attack
W - 7. ROBESON	G.	What Brian's parents had gotten
A - 8. RASPBERRIES	H.	Brian's age
K - 9. DREAMS	I.	Brian built one to store the fresh fish
Y - 10. TORNADO	J.	Plane crashed into it
J - 11. LAKE	K.	They helped Brian think of ways to survive
F - 12. BEAR	L.	Brian unknowingly activated the emergency one
D - 13. FLOATS	M.	Brian got the ___ pack from the back of the plane
E - 14. MOSQUITOES	N.	The senseless attack of this animal drove Brian into the water
Q - 15. HUNGER	O.	Brian used a ___ and arrows to kill the rabbits
B - 16. AMBER	P.	Teenage wilderness survivor
V - 17. TERRY	Q.	It drove Brian to hunt
N - 18. MOOSE	R.	First Meat
M - 19. SURVIVAL	S.	Model of the plane that crashed
P - 20. BRIAN	T.	The ___ buyer rescued Brian
I - 21. POND	U.	The ___ plane didn't see Brian and turned away
S - 22. CESSNA	V.	Pretended to be lost in the woods with Brian
C - 23. TOUGH	W.	Mr. ___ worked in the oil fields in Canada
R - 24. FOOLBIRD	X.	Attack of this animal caused Brian to create fire
H - 25. THIRTEEN	Y.	It destroyed Brian's shelter

Hatchet Matching 3

___ 1. DREAMS   A. Teacher who told students to value themselves
___ 2. SECRET   B. Brian's second food
___ 3. CANADA   C. Attack of this animal caused Brian to create fire
___ 4. AMBER   D. Mall where Brian saw his mother and the other man
___ 5. TOUGH   E. That Brian knew he could learn and survive was ___ Hope
___ 6. MOSQUITOES   F. Number of days Brian spent in the wilderness
___ 7. FOOLBIRD   G. They made a living coat on Brian's skin
___ 8. HATCHET   H. Author
___ 9. SEARCH   I. What Brian's parents had gotten
___10. DIVORCE   J. Brian got the ___ pack from the back of the plane
___11. CHERRIES   K. Brian's age
___12. YORK   L. Plane crashed into it
___13. PILOT   M. The ___ buyer rescued Brian
___14. TWO   N. Number of hours Brian was blinded by the skunk
___15. PERPICH   O. They helped Brian think of ways to survive
___16. PORCUPINE   P. Where Brian was going
___17. LAKE   Q. Brian's first food
___18. SURVIVAL   R. Plane started out in New ___
___19. THIRTEEN   S. He died of a heart attack
___20. BEAR   T. Gift from Brian's mother
___21. PAULSEN   U. First Meat
___22. FUR   V. It saw Brian near the berry bushes but did not attack
___23. BRIAN   W. Teenage wilderness survivor
___24. RASPBERRIES   X. The ___ was that Brian saw his mother with another man
___25. FIFTYFOUR   Y. The ___ plane didn't see Brian and turned away

Hatchet Matching 3 Answer Key

O - 1. DREAMS   A. Teacher who told students to value themselves
X - 2. SECRET   B. Brian's second food
P - 3. CANADA   C. Attack of this animal caused Brian to create fire
D - 4. AMBER   D. Mall where Brian saw his mother and the other man
E - 5. TOUGH   E. That Brian knew he could learn and survive was ___ Hope
G - 6. MOSQUITOES   F. Number of days Brian spent in the wilderness
U - 7. FOOLBIRD   G. They made a living coat on Brian's skin
T - 8. HATCHET   H. Author
Y - 9. SEARCH   I. What Brian's parents had gotten
I - 10. DIVORCE   J. Brian got the ___ pack from the back of the plane
Q - 11. CHERRIES   K. Brian's age
R - 12. YORK   L. Plane crashed into it
S - 13. PILOT   M. The ___ buyer rescued Brian
N - 14. TWO   N. Number of hours Brian was blinded by the skunk
A - 15. PERPICH   O. They helped Brian think of ways to survive
C - 16. PORCUPINE   P. Where Brian was going
L - 17. LAKE   Q. Brian's first food
J - 18. SURVIVAL   R. Plane started out in New ___
K - 19. THIRTEEN   S. He died of a heart attack
V - 20. BEAR   T. Gift from Brian's mother
H - 21. PAULSEN   U. First Meat
M - 22. FUR   V. It saw Brian near the berry bushes but did not attack
W - 23. BRIAN   W. Teenage wilderness survivor
B - 24. RASPBERRIES   X. The ___ was that Brian saw his mother with another man
F - 25. FIFTYFOUR   Y. The ___ plane didn't see Brian and turned away

Hatchet Matching 4

___ 1. YORK   A. The ___ was that Brian saw his mother with another man
___ 2. DREAMS   B. That Brian knew he could learn and survive was ___ Hope
___ 3. PORCUPINE   C. He died of a heart attack
___ 4. BEAR   D. Mr. ___ worked in the oil fields in Canada
___ 5. FLOATS   E. The plane that rescued Brian had these
___ 6. POND   F. Plane started out in New ___
___ 7. THIRTEEN   G. Brian took its eggs for food
___ 8. ROBESON   H. Brian unknowingly activated the emergency one
___ 9. PAULSEN   I. Teenage wilderness survivor
___10. SECRET   J. Model of the plane that crashed
___11. CESSNA   K. Brian's first food
___12. BRIAN   L. Gift from Brian's mother
___13. HATCHET   M. Where Brian stored his food after the skunk got the eggs
___14. TURTLE   N. Attack of this animal caused Brian to create fire
___15. LEDGE   O. It destroyed Brian's shelter
___16. RASPBERRIES   P. Interested in Brian for a few months upon his return
___17. CHERRIES   Q. They helped Brian think of ways to survive
___18. TOUGH   R. Pretended to be lost in the woods with Brian
___19. PRESS   S. Brian built one to store the fresh fish
___20. CANADA   T. Brian's second food
___21. PILOT   U. Brian's age
___22. TORNADO   V. Plane crashed into it
___23. LAKE   W. It saw Brian near the berry bushes but did not attack
___24. TRANSMITTER   X. Author
___25. TERRY   Y. Where Brian was going

Hatchet Matching 4 Answer Key

F - 1. YORK	A.	The ___ was that Brian saw his mother with another man
Q - 2. DREAMS	B.	That Brian knew he could learn and survive was ___ Hope
N - 3. PORCUPINE	C.	He died of a heart attack
W - 4. BEAR	D.	Mr. ___ worked in the oil fields in Canada
E - 5. FLOATS	E.	The plane that rescued Brian had these
S - 6. POND	F.	Plane started out in New ___
U - 7. THIRTEEN	G.	Brian took its eggs for food
D - 8. ROBESON	H.	Brian unknowingly activated the emergency one
X - 9. PAULSEN	I.	Teenage wilderness survivor
A - 10. SECRET	J.	Model of the plane that crashed
J - 11. CESSNA	K.	Brian's first food
I - 12. BRIAN	L.	Gift from Brian's mother
L - 13. HATCHET	M.	Where Brian stored his food after the skunk got the eggs
G - 14. TURTLE	N.	Attack of this animal caused Brian to create fire
M - 15. LEDGE	O.	It destroyed Brian's shelter
T - 16. RASPBERRIES	P.	Interested in Brian for a few months upon his return
K - 17. CHERRIES	Q.	They helped Brian think of ways to survive
B - 18. TOUGH	R.	Pretended to be lost in the woods with Brian
P - 19. PRESS	S.	Brian built one to store the fresh fish
Y - 20. CANADA	T.	Brian's second food
C - 21. PILOT	U.	Brian's age
O - 22. TORNADO	V.	Plane crashed into it
V - 23. LAKE	W.	It saw Brian near the berry bushes but did not attack
H - 24. TRANSMITTER	X.	Author
R - 25. TERRY	Y.	Where Brian was going

Hatchet Magic Squares 1

Match the definition with the vocabulary word. Put your answers in the magic squares below. When your answers are correct, all columns and rows will add to the same number.

A. SURVIVAL   E. TORNADO   I. TURTLE   M. FUR
B. DREAMS   F. SEARCH   J. TRANSMITTER   N. TOUGH
C. CHERRIES   G. DIVORCE   K. BRUSHPILE   O. HATCHET
D. MOSQUITOES   H. FIFTYFOUR   L. PRESS   P. CANADA

1. Number of days Brian spent in the wilderness
2. Brian got the ___ pack from the back of the plane
3. They helped Brian think of ways to survive
4. What Brian's parents had gotten
5. Brian unknowingly activated the emergency one
6. Gift from Brian's mother
7. Where Brian was going
8. Brian took its eggs for food
9. Raft Brian built to get to the plane: ___ One
10. That Brian knew he could learn and survive was ___ Hope
11. The ___ buyer rescued Brian
12. Interested in Brian for a few months upon his return
13. It destroyed Brian's shelter
14. They made a living coat on Brian's skin
15. Brian's first food
16. The ___ plane didn't see Brian and turned away

A=	B=	C=	D=
E=	F=	G=	H=
I=	J=	K=	L=
M=	N=	O=	P=

Hatchet Magic Squares 1 Answer Key

Match the definition with the vocabulary word. Put your answers in the magic squares below. When your answers are correct, all columns and rows will add to the same number.

A. SURVIVAL E. TORNADO I. TURTLE M. FUR
B. DREAMS F. SEARCH J. TRANSMITTER N. TOUGH
C. CHERRIES G. DIVORCE K. BRUSHPILE O. HATCHET
D. MOSQUITOES H. FIFTYFOUR L. PRESS P. CANADA

1. Number of days Brian spent in the wilderness
2. Brian got the ___ pack from the back of the plane
3. They helped Brian think of ways to survive
4. What Brian's parents had gotten
5. Brian unknowingly activated the emergency one
6. Gift from Brian's mother
7. Where Brian was going
8. Brian took its eggs for food
9. Raft Brian built to get to the plane: ___ One
10. That Brian knew he could learn and survive was ___ Hope
11. The ___ buyer rescued Brian
12. Interested in Brian for a few months upon his return
13. It destroyed Brian's shelter
14. They made a living coat on Brian's skin
15. Brian's first food
16. The ___ plane didn't see Brian and turned away

A=2	B=3	C=15	D=14
E=13	F=16	G=4	H=1
I=8	J=5	K=9	L=12
M=11	N=10	O=6	P=7

Hatchet Magic Squares 2

Match the definition with the vocabulary word. Put your answers in the magic squares below. When your answers are correct, all columns and rows will add to the same number.

A. FLOATS
B. BOW
C. PRESS
D. TURTLE
E. FUR
F. AMBER
G. TWO
H. YORK
I. RASPBERRIES
J. PORCUPINE
K. PILOT
L. HATCHET
M. LEDGE
N. MOOSE
O. HUNGER
P. ROBESON

1. Brian used a ___ and arrows to kill the rabbits
2. Number of hours Brian was blinded by the skunk
3. He died of a heart attack
4. The senseless attack of this animal drove Brian into the water
5. Where Brian stored his food after the skunk got the eggs
6. Gift from Brian's mother
7. Plane started out in New ___
8. The plane that rescued Brian had these
9. Mr. ___ worked in the oil fields in Canada
10. Brian's second food
11. The ___ buyer rescued Brian
12. Brian took its eggs for food
13. Interested in Brian for a few months upon his return
14. Mall where Brian saw his mother and the other man
15. Attack of this animal caused Brian to create fire
16. It drove Brian to hunt

A=	B=	C=	D=
E=	F=	G=	H=
I=	J=	K=	L=
M=	N=	O=	P=

Hatchet Magic Squares 2 Answer Key

Match the definition with the vocabulary word. Put your answers in the magic squares below. When your answers are correct, all columns and rows will add to the same number.

A. FLOATS
B. BOW
C. PRESS
D. TURTLE
E. FUR
F. AMBER
G. TWO
H. YORK
I. RASPBERRIES
J. PORCUPINE
K. PILOT
L. HATCHET
M. LEDGE
N. MOOSE
O. HUNGER
P. ROBESON

1. Brian used a ___ and arrows to kill the rabbits
2. Number of hours Brian was blinded by the skunk
3. He died of a heart attack
4. The senseless attack of this animal drove Brian into the water
5. Where Brian stored his food after the skunk got the eggs
6. Gift from Brian's mother
7. Plane started out in New ___
8. The plane that rescued Brian had these
9. Mr. ___ worked in the oil fields in Canada
10. Brian's second food
11. The ___ buyer rescued Brian
12. Brian took its eggs for food
13. Interested in Brian for a few months upon his return
14. Mall where Brian saw his mother and the other man
15. Attack of this animal caused Brian to create fire
16. It drove Brian to hunt

A=8	B=1	C=13	D=12
E=11	F=14	G=2	H=7
I=10	J=15	K=3	L=6
M=5	N=4	O=16	P=9

Hatchet Magic Squares 3

Match the definition with the vocabulary word. Put your answers in the magic squares below. When your answers are correct, all columns and rows will add to the same number.

A. FIRE
B. HUNGER
C. POND
D. BRUSHPILE
E. PAULSEN
F. MOOSE
G. MOSQUITOES
H. RASPBERRIES
I. PORCUPINE
J. SEARCH
K. SECRET
L. FIFTYFOUR
M. DIVORCE
N. TERRY
O. CANADA
P. YORK

1. The senseless attack of this animal drove Brian into the water
2. Attack of this animal caused Brian to create fire
3. Where Brian was going
4. Raft Brian built to get to the plane: ___ One
5. What Brian's parents had gotten
6. It drove Brian to hunt
7. Brian's second food
8. The ___ was that Brian saw his mother with another man
9. Brian built one to store the fresh fish
10. Plane started out in New ___
11. The ___ plane didn't see Brian and turned away
12. Author
13. Number of days Brian spent in the wilderness
14. They made a living coat on Brian's skin
15. Friend that Brian created
16. Pretended to be lost in the woods with Brian

A=	B=	C=	D=
E=	F=	G=	H=
I=	J=	K=	L=
M=	N=	O=	P=

Hatchet Magic Squares 3 Answer Key

Match the definition with the vocabulary word. Put your answers in the magic squares below. When your answers are correct, all columns and rows will add to the same number.

A. FIRE
B. HUNGER
C. POND
D. BRUSHPILE
E. PAULSEN
F. MOOSE
G. MOSQUITOES
H. RASPBERRIES
I. PORCUPINE
J. SEARCH
K. SECRET
L. FIFTYFOUR
M. DIVORCE
N. TERRY
O. CANADA
P. YORK

1. The senseless attack of this animal drove Brian into the water
2. Attack of this animal caused Brian to create fire
3. Where Brian was going
4. Raft Brian built to get to the plane: ___ One
5. What Brian's parents had gotten
6. It drove Brian to hunt
7. Brian's second food
8. The ___ was that Brian saw his mother with another man
9. Brian built one to store the fresh fish
10. Plane started out in New ___
11. The ___ plane didn't see Brian and turned away
12. Author
13. Number of days Brian spent in the wilderness
14. They made a living coat on Brian's skin
15. Friend that Brian created
16. Pretended to be lost in the woods with Brian

A=15	B=6	C=9	D=4
E=12	F=1	G=14	H=7
I=2	J=11	K=8	L=13
M=5	N=16	O=3	P=10

Hatchet Magic Squares 4

Match the definition with the vocabulary word. Put your answers in the magic squares below. When your answers are correct, all columns and rows will add to the same number.

A. DREAMS
B. YORK
C. TOUGH
D. LAKE
E. LEDGE
F. PRESS
G. FIRE
H. PAULSEN
I. BEAR
J. FOOLBIRD
K. TORNADO
L. TURTLE
M. SEARCH
N. HATCHET
O. FIFTYFOUR
P. SECRET

1. They helped Brian think of ways to survive
2. Gift from Brian's mother
3. First Meat
4. Where Brian stored his food after the skunk got the eggs
5. Friend that Brian created
6. Brian took its eggs for food
7. The ___ was that Brian saw his mother with another man
8. That Brian knew he could learn and survive was ___ Hope
9. Number of days Brian spent in the wilderness
10. Plane crashed into it
11. Author
12. It destroyed Brian's shelter
13. It saw Brian near the berry bushes but did not attack
14. Interested in Brian for a few months upon his return
15. Plane started out in New ___
16. The ___ plane didn't see Brian and turned away

A=	B=	C=	D=
E=	F=	G=	H=
I=	J=	K=	L=
M=	N=	O=	P=

Hatchet Magic Squares 4 Answer Key

Match the definition with the vocabulary word. Put your answers in the magic squares below. When your answers are correct, all columns and rows will add to the same number.

A. DREAMS
B. YORK
C. TOUGH
D. LAKE
E. LEDGE
F. PRESS
G. FIRE
H. PAULSEN
I. BEAR
J. FOOLBIRD
K. TORNADO
L. TURTLE
M. SEARCH
N. HATCHET
O. FIFTYFOUR
P. SECRET

1. They helped Brian think of ways to survive
2. Gift from Brian's mother
3. First Meat
4. Where Brian stored his food after the skunk got the eggs
5. Friend that Brian created
6. Brian took its eggs for food
7. The ___ was that Brian saw his mother with another man
8. That Brian knew he could learn and survive was ___ Hope
9. Number of days Brian spent in the wilderness
10. Plane crashed into it
11. Author
12. It destroyed Brian's shelter
13. It saw Brian near the berry bushes but did not attack
14. Interested in Brian for a few months upon his return
15. Plane started out in New ___
16. The ___ plane didn't see Brian and turned away

A=1	B=15	C=8	D=10
E=4	F=14	G=5	H=11
I=13	J=3	K=12	L=6
M=16	N=2	O=9	P=7

Hatchet Word Search 1

```
H C H D L J O R P Y M L P P D G Q Y H
R Y H D I D G B E W H S R R P Q D P K
L C R E A V Q J R Y R E T R U F K W
C S X N R F O C P Y K A S C S I L F N
Z T R L Q R K R I K M M S N R W O O L
C O Y V B R I J C S J K Y E Y E A O N
T E S O O M W E H E M R D J R H T L J
L R C Y W P X P S T G N T Z E N S B J
T S A B B M X K B C O D U T G F C I R
B E L N M R B F R P M W R W N K B R A
L A K E S U R V I V A L T O U G H D S
P R M T D M D Y A F X Z L W H H R S P
G C P B H G I Q N H T X E R O Y P P B
C H L I E I E T R W A Y C A N A D A E
Z E C M L R R A T D H T F B N F Z U R
S N S L P O E T Y E V X C O B J D L R
K M M S C B T M E D R W B H U Y F S I
C X C H N R R O B E S O N J E R R E E
R C F W J A K T S Y N R T X B T Y N S
```

Author (7)
Brian built one to store the fresh fish (4)
Brian got the ___ pack from the back of the plane (8)
Brian took its eggs for food (6)
Brian unknowingly activated the emergency one (11)
Brian used a ___ and arrows to kill the rabbits (3)
Brian's age (8)
Brian's first food (8)
Brian's second food (11)
First Meat (8)
Friend that Brian created (4)
Gift from Brian's mother (7)
He died of a heart attack (5)
Interested in Brian for a few months upon his return (5)
It destroyed Brian's shelter (7)
It drove Brian to hunt (6)
It saw Brian near the berry bushes but did not attack (4)
Mall where Brian saw his mother and the other man (5)
Model of the plane that crashed (6)
Mr. ___ worked in the oil fields in Canada (7)
Number of days Brian spent in the wilderness (9)
Number of hours Brian was blinded by the skunk (3)
Plane crashed into it (4)
Plane started out in New ___ (4)
Pretended to be lost in the woods with Brian (5)
Teacher who told students to value themselves (7)
Teenage wilderness survivor (5)
That Brian knew he could learn and survive was ___ Hope (5)
The ___ buyer rescued Brian (3)
The ___ plane didn't see Brian and turned away (6)
The ___ was that Brian saw his mother with another man (6)
The plane that rescued Brian had these (6)
The senseless attack of this animal drove Brian into the water (5)
They helped Brian think of ways to survive (6)
What Brian's parents had gotten (7)
Where Brian stored his food after the skunk got the eggs (5)
Where Brian was going (6)

Hatchet Word Search 1 Answer Key

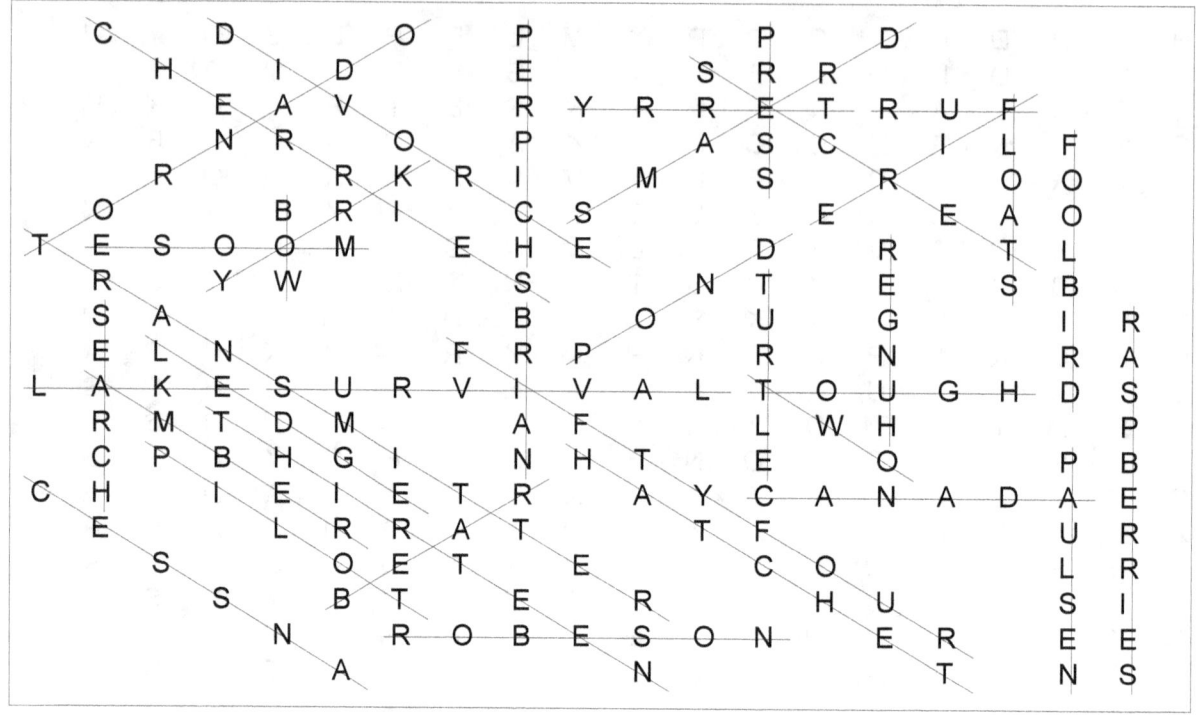

Author (7)
Brian built one to store the fresh fish (4)
Brian got the ___ pack from the back of the plane (8)
Brian took its eggs for food (6)
Brian unknowingly activated the emergency one (11)
Brian used a ___ and arrows to kill the rabbits (3)
Brian's age (8)
Brian's first food (8)
Brian's second food (11)
First Meat (8)
Friend that Brian created (4)
Gift from Brian's mother (7)
He died of a heart attack (5)
Interested in Brian for a few months upon his return (5)
It destroyed Brian's shelter (7)
It drove Brian to hunt (6)
It saw Brian near the berry bushes but did not attack (4)
Mall where Brian saw his mother and the other man (5)
Model of the plane that crashed (6)
Mr. ___ worked in the oil fields in Canada (7)
Number of days Brian spent in the wilderness (9)
Number of hours Brian was blinded by the skunk (3)
Plane crashed into it (4)
Plane started out in New ___ (4)
Pretended to be lost in the woods with Brian (5)
Teacher who told students to value themselves (7)
Teenage wilderness survivor (5)
That Brian knew he could learn and survive was ___ Hope (5)
The ___ buyer rescued Brian (3)
The ___ plane didn't see Brian and turned away (6)
The ___ was that Brian saw his mother with another man (6)
The plane that rescued Brian had these (6)
The senseless attack of this animal drove Brian into the water (5)
They helped Brian think of ways to survive (6)
What Brian's parents had gotten (7)
Where Brian stored his food after the skunk got the eggs (5)
Where Brian was going (6)

Hatchet Word Search 2

```
R S F G X V X T C H E R R I E S M H W
O C O V G B X T H Q J D M L T K C L G
B Y O R F Z Q T H I K T O D J I J H Y
E F L T Y V G F N D R D O H P W X V F
S S B K V N F G U H P T S R C S F R K
O F I F T Y F O U R I R E G N U H W R
N X R S K L H I P K L P W E P A O K E
B M D Y F S G R R D O L S K N B D R T
T E R B B D E G Z E T L F A B T H O T
W Z A N S S E C E T U R T L E R S Y I
O L S R S M E G Q A T G P H O E I M M
Z W P X B A D A P Y L X C D O A G A S
A M B E R E N Y R A G T V T W Z T W N
M S E H L R O C V C A F I E E K J S A
D S R V T D P I A H H U V R T R Y Q R
N X R Q J J V D R N Q S P C Q O R J T
R D I V O R C E M S A Y J E T R U Y K
V D E F U G T V O K K D M S R M F G H
Q C S S H T Q M P R H T A C K W N Y H
```

Author (7)
Brian built one to store the fresh fish (4)
Brian got the ___ pack from the back of the plane (8)
Brian took its eggs for food (6)
Brian unknowingly activated the emergency one (11)
Brian used a ___ and arrows to kill the rabbits (3)
Brian's age (8)
Brian's first food (8)
Brian's second food (11)
First Meat (8)
Friend that Brian created (4)
Gift from Brian's mother (7)
He died of a heart attack (5)
Interested in Brian for a few months upon his return (5)
It destroyed Brian's shelter (7)
It drove Brian to hunt (6)
It saw Brian near the berry bushes but did not attack (4)
Mall where Brian saw his mother and the other man (5)
Model of the plane that crashed (6)
Mr. ___ worked in the oil fields in Canada (7)
Number of days Brian spent in the wilderness (9)
Number of hours Brian was blinded by the skunk (3)
Plane crashed into it (4)
Plane started out in New ___ (4)
Pretended to be lost in the woods with Brian (5)
Teacher who told students to value themselves (7)
Teenage wilderness survivor (5)
That Brian knew he could learn and survive was ___ Hope (5)
The ___ buyer rescued Brian (3)
The ___ plane didn't see Brian and turned away (6)
The ___ was that Brian saw his mother with another man (6)
The plane that rescued Brian had these (6)
The senseless attack of this animal drove Brian into the water (5)
They helped Brian think of ways to survive (6)
They made a living coat on Brian's skin (10)
What Brian's parents had gotten (7)
Where Brian stored his food after the skunk got the eggs (5)
Where Brian was going (6)

Hatchet Word Search 2 Answer Key

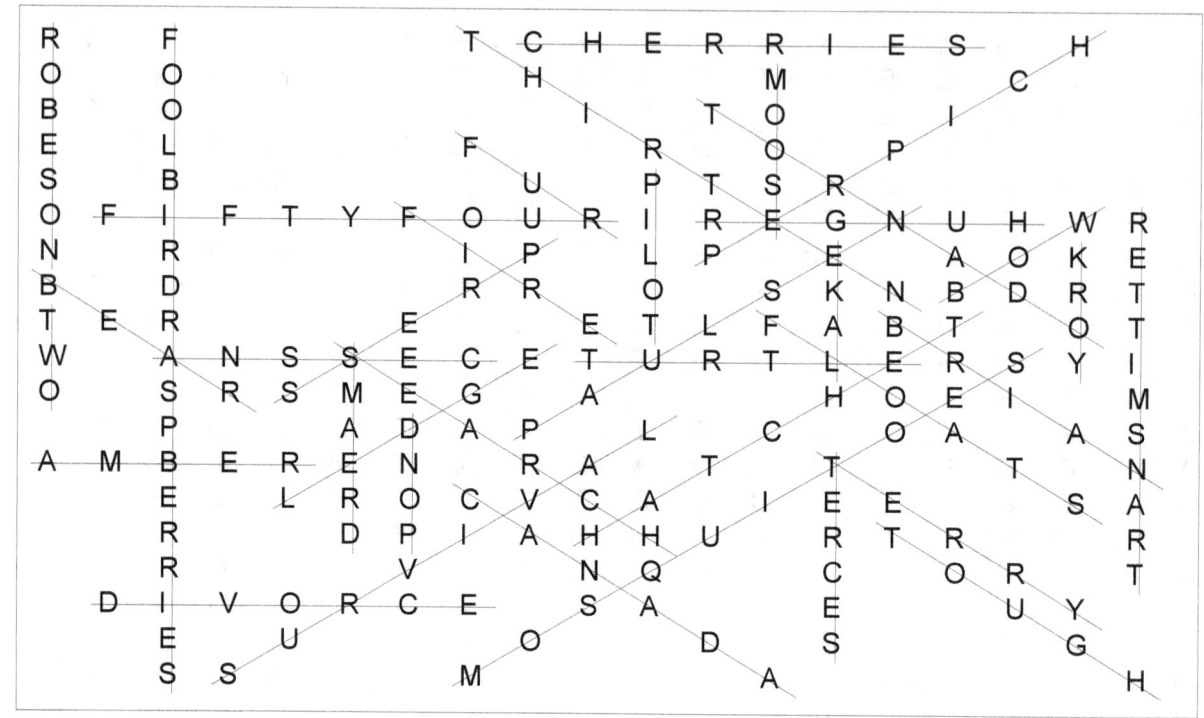

Author (7)
Brian built one to store the fresh fish (4)
Brian got the ___ pack from the back of the plane (8)
Brian took its eggs for food (6)
Brian unknowingly activated the emergency one (11)
Brian used a ___ and arrows to kill the rabbits (3)
Brian's age (8)
Brian's first food (8)
Brian's second food (11)
First Meat (8)
Friend that Brian created (4)
Gift from Brian's mother (7)
He died of a heart attack (5)
Interested in Brian for a few months upon his return (5)
It destroyed Brian's shelter (7)
It drove Brian to hunt (6)
It saw Brian near the berry bushes but did not attack (4)
Mall where Brian saw his mother and the other man (5)
Model of the plane that crashed (6)
Mr. ___ worked in the oil fields in Canada (7)
Number of days Brian spent in the wilderness (9)
Number of hours Brian was blinded by the skunk (3)
Plane crashed into it (4)
Plane started out in New ___ (4)
Pretended to be lost in the woods with Brian (5)
Teacher who told students to value themselves (7)
Teenage wilderness survivor (5)
That Brian knew he could learn and survive was ___ Hope (5)
The ___ buyer rescued Brian (3)
The ___ plane didn't see Brian and turned away (6)
The ___ was that Brian saw his mother with another man (6)
The plane that rescued Brian had these (6)
The senseless attack of this animal drove Brian into the water (5)
They helped Brian think of ways to survive (6)
They made a living coat on Brian's skin (10)
What Brian's parents had gotten (7)
Where Brian stored his food after the skunk got the eggs (5)
Where Brian was going (6)

Hatchet Word Search 3

```
B M O O S E S U R V I V A L H P Y M P N
O R G S Y K S H X F F Q T V X R X O N S
W T I Z J C B E F K N R F M R Z X S R F
M V H A G G C M A X P O B E G F M Q W K
V A D A N A C V P R O W T E L T R U T K
X S N I C D K R U L C O O N B E N I P Y
M T O L V H R F B G L H R B E R P T Z J
K A P P M O E I P I K E N N A C N O R J
N O S E B O R R P H M L A V R E J E P M
Z L D S R D T C R Y F I D F X S G S I L
V F N W A F C F E I P P O W J D J Z C W
Q I X Y S P M M H D E H K P E Y V T H V
M R B Z P K P H N R M S N L F M G Q X Y
B E L P B Z X H R E S U S L T Q W S B R
M B C O E G R Z F A B R S Q S Q H X E C
W K G R V X S C M Y B M T P H Q T F K
M Y B C R J J M N S M T R F L M T V I M
R X Q U I T J T N D D E B R C I B G F X
R P T P E D X O Q P G H B G M M V F T C
C P X I S T N U V N B C C S D T Y H Y S
D N R N R L X G U T L T N E S R S H F B
G N E E T R I H T M P A U L S E N Q O L
J S B W S W B J Q L R H K L X S D G U L
C M M F S S D H S T Y G W E B V N R R Y
A M X J D Q M J T G Q M W Z X Z N A J D
```

AMBER	DIVORCE	HUNGER	POND	TERRY
BEAR	DREAMS	LAKE	PORCUPINE	THIRTEEN
BOW	FIFTYFOUR	LEDGE	PRESS	TORNADO
BRIAN	FIRE	MOOSE	RASPBERRIES	TOUGH
BRUSHPILE	FLOATS	MOSQUITOES	ROBESON	TRANSMITTER
CANADA	FOOLBIRD	PAULSEN	SEARCH	TURTLE
CESSNA	FUR	PERPICH	SECRET	TWO
CHERRIES	HATCHET	PILOT	SURVIVAL	YORK

Hatchet Word Search 3 Answer Key

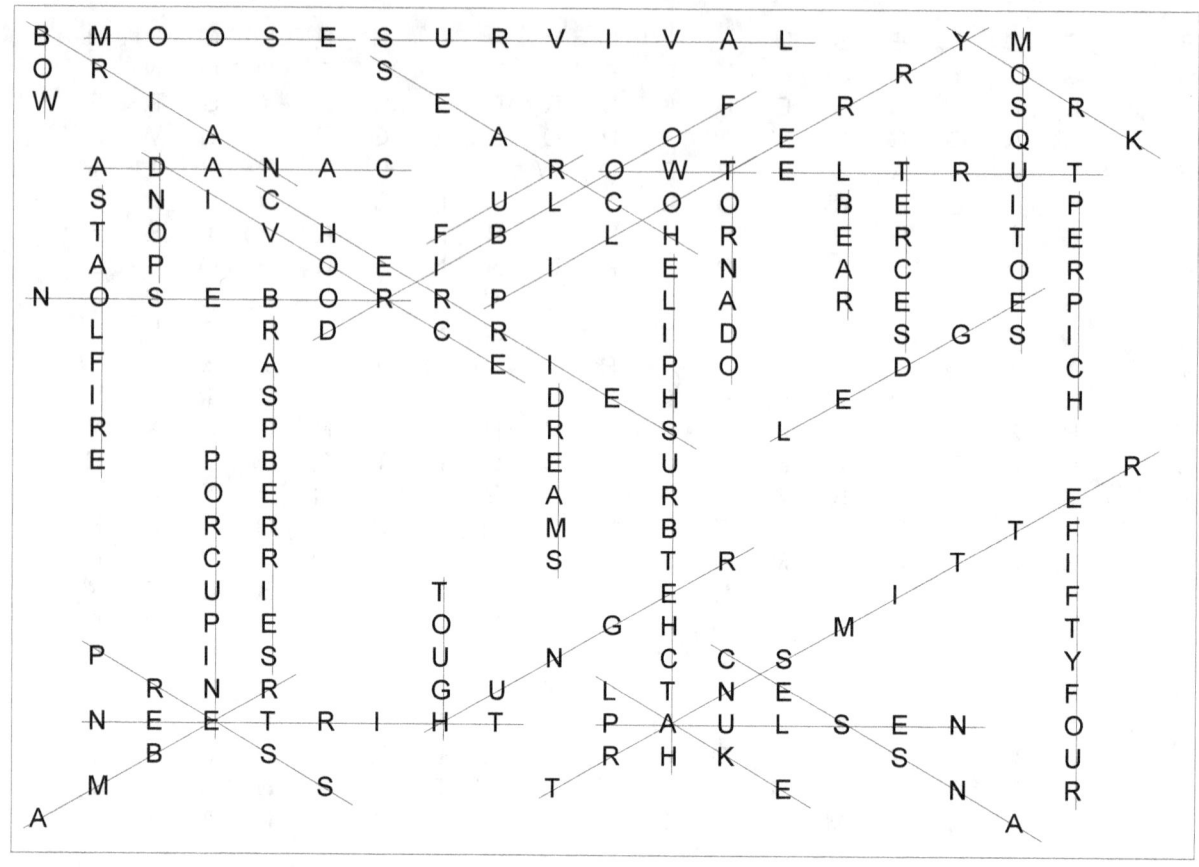

AMBER	DIVORCE	HUNGER	POND	TERRY
BEAR	DREAMS	LAKE	PORCUPINE	THIRTEEN
BOW	FIFTYFOUR	LEDGE	PRESS	TORNADO
BRIAN	FIRE	MOOSE	RASPBERRIES	TOUGH
BRUSHPILE	FLOATS	MOSQUITOES	ROBESON	TRANSMITTER
CANADA	FOOLBIRD	PAULSEN	SEARCH	TURTLE
CESSNA	FUR	PERPICH	SECRET	TWO
CHERRIES	HATCHET	PILOT	SURVIVAL	YORK

Hatchet Word Search 4

```
Z D R F C F H R L T D Z W T P B V X K X
B P O Z I E N A R X H D P K D W R V M C
T X B R L T S P T J T P R R D V P I R R
L S E C R E T S H C R A E S Y O R K A W
S D S Z C R D Z N U H A S R N K G E S N
Y D O L Q R Q G O A M E S D P W B V P B
T Z N N A Y R F E S G B T G Q I K Z B K
T O U G H K Y L C H E R R I E S C E E C
T T R X Y T E A R S Q U M U U G S H R P
Z U Z N F T N F O J Q F X R S O Z B R H
C R T I A A W O V J H K V A O H S B I C
J T F P D D N O I Q T I F M P Q P C E Y
G L V A R T O L D O V P O B S H X I S Y
B E R U Z N H B L A L S O E D R Q N L C
C F L L B O W I L T Q J R R E G N U H E
K L M S V T P R R U H L W T C L R P X Y
P O X E R X G D I T D J T N N U H H X T
B A T N G H F T Q P E I B V M G P X F C
S T N X M Q O P Z V M E F Q C C D I J W
J S J D Q E N W X S Q N N H M X G S N C
V Y S D S R C S N B L D H V K K N C E
X H R T M Z R A K C M X M Q M V R N R R
S C L Z R H R W C F T J N P M V D J T Q
S V C H F T F Q Z L W F W G J V V K K R
D K C G K C M V Y Q M L G F K Z M V M V
```

AMBER	DIVORCE	HUNGER	POND	TERRY
BEAR	DREAMS	LAKE	PORCUPINE	THIRTEEN
BOW	FIFTYFOUR	LEDGE	PRESS	TORNADO
BRIAN	FIRE	MOOSE	RASPBERRIES	TOUGH
BRUSHPILE	FLOATS	MOSQUITOES	ROBESON	TRANSMITTER
CANADA	FOOLBIRD	PAULSEN	SEARCH	TURTLE
CESSNA	FUR	PERPICH	SECRET	TWO
CHERRIES	HATCHET	PILOT	SURVIVAL	YORK

Hatchet Word Search 4 Answer Key

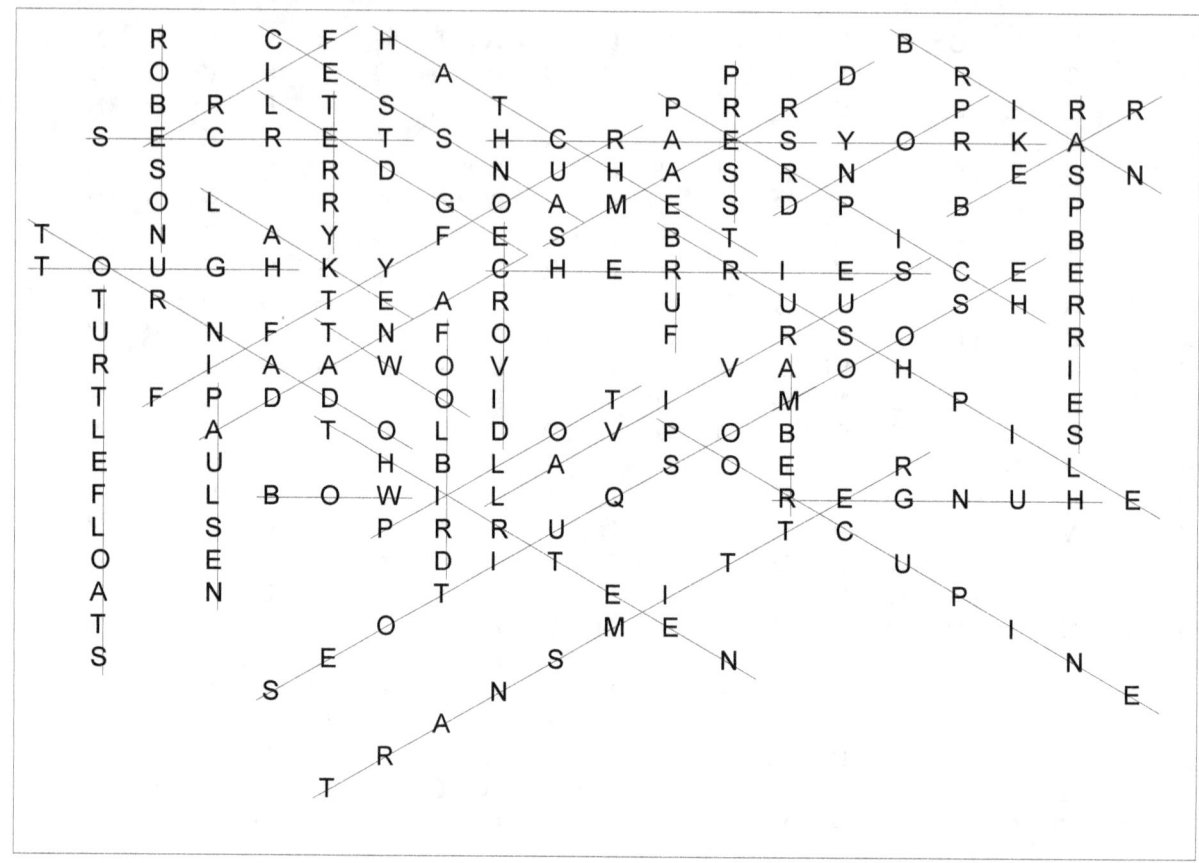

AMBER	DIVORCE	HUNGER	POND	TERRY
BEAR	DREAMS	LAKE	PORCUPINE	THIRTEEN
BOW	FIFTYFOUR	LEDGE	PRESS	TORNADO
BRIAN	FIRE	MOOSE	RASPBERRIES	TOUGH
BRUSHPILE	FLOATS	MOSQUITOES	ROBESON	TRANSMITTER
CANADA	FOOLBIRD	PAULSEN	SEARCH	TURTLE
CESSNA	FUR	PERPICH	SECRET	TWO
CHERRIES	HATCHET	PILOT	SURVIVAL	YORK

Hatchet Crossword 1

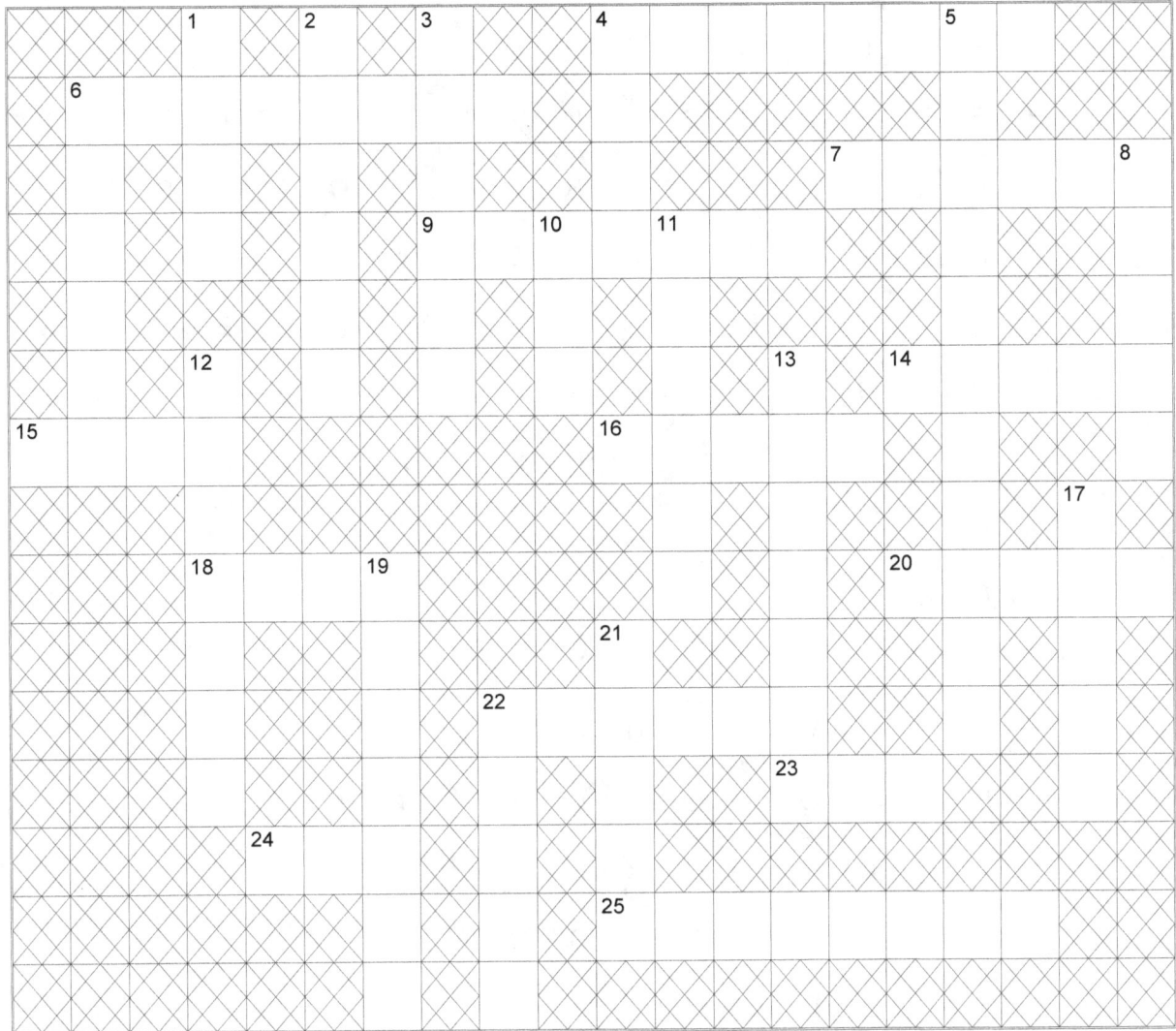

Across
4. First Meat
6. Brian's first food
7. Model of the plane that crashed
9. Mr. ___ worked in the oil fields in Canada
14. Where Brian stored his food after the skunk got the eggs
15. Plane crashed into it
16. Teenage wilderness survivor
18. Brian built one to store the fresh fish
20. He died of a heart attack
22. Brian took its eggs for food
23. Number of hours Brian was blinded by the skunk
24. The ___ buyer rescued Brian
25. Brian got the ___ pack from the back of the plane

Down
1. It saw Brian near the berry bushes but did not attack
2. They helped Brian think of ways to survive
3. The ___ was that Brian saw his mother with another man
4. Friend that Brian created
5. Brian's second food
6. Where Brian was going
8. Mall where Brian saw his mother and the other man
10. Brian used a ___ and arrows to kill the rabbits
11. The ___ plane didn't see Brian and turned away
12. Teacher who told students to value themselves
13. Gift from Brian's mother
17. The senseless attack of this animal drove Brian into the water
19. What Brian's parents had gotten
21. Interested in Brian for a few months upon his return
22. That Brian knew he could learn and survive was ___ Hope

Hatchet Crossword 1 Answer Key

```
    1 B    2 D    3 S         4 F  O  O  L  B  I  R  D
 6 C  H  E  R  R  I  E  S     I                    A
    A     A     E     C       R           7 C  E  S  S  N  A  8
    N     R     A    9 R  10 O  11 B  E  S  O  N     P           M
    A           M    E     O     E                  B           B
    D    12 P   S    T     W     A    13 H  14 L  E  D  G  E
15 L  A  K  E              16 B  R  I  A  N     R
          R                       C     T           R     17 M
       18 P  O  19 N  D                 H     C    20 P  I  L  O  T
          I        I                          H        E        O
          C        V      22 T  U  R  21 P  L        S        S
          H        O      T              H   23 T  W  O        E
                24 F  U  R     O              E
                            U             25 S  U  R  V  I  V  A  L
                              E
                              G
                              H
```

Across

4. First Meat
6. Brian's first food
7. Model of the plane that crashed
9. Mr. ___ worked in the oil fields in Canada
14. Where Brian stored his food after the skunk got the eggs
15. Plane crashed into it
16. Teenage wilderness survivor
18. Brian built one to store the fresh fish
20. He died of a heart attack
22. Brian took its eggs for food
23. Number of hours Brian was blinded by the skunk
24. The ___ buyer rescued Brian
25. Brian got the ___ pack from the back of the plane

Down

1. It saw Brian near the berry bushes but did not attack
2. They helped Brian think of ways to survive
3. The ___ was that Brian saw his mother with another man
4. Friend that Brian created
5. Brian's second food
6. Where Brian was going
8. Mall where Brian saw his mother and the other man
10. Brian used a ___ and arrows to kill the rabbits
11. The ___ plane didn't see Brian and turned away
12. Teacher who told students to value themselves
13. Gift from Brian's mother
17. The senseless attack of this animal drove Brian into the water
19. What Brian's parents had gotten
21. Interested in Brian for a few months upon his return
22. That Brian knew he could learn and survive was ___ Hope

Hatchet Crossword 2

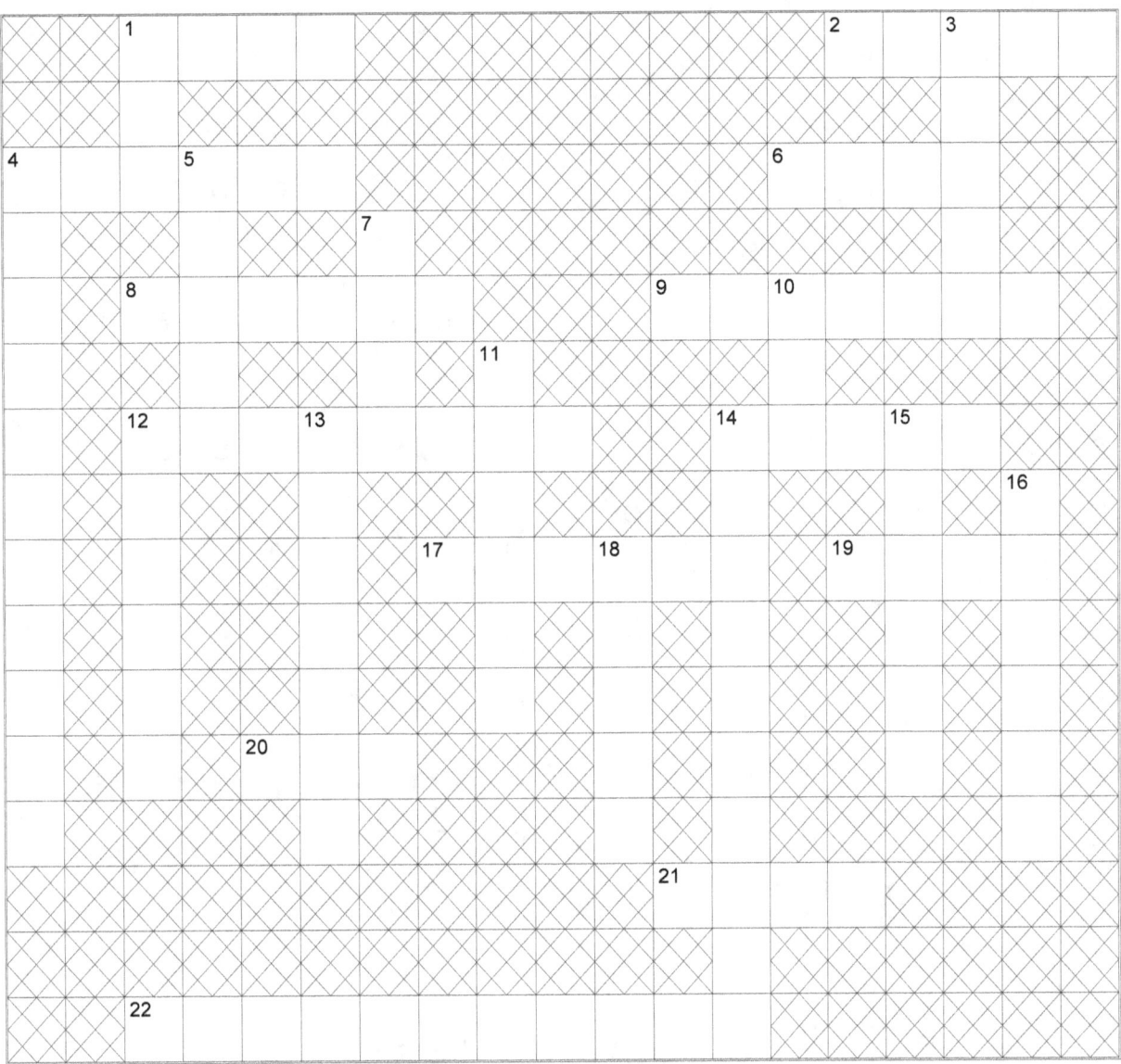

Across
1. Friend that Brian created
2. He died of a heart attack
4. Brian took its eggs for food
6. Brian built one to store the fresh fish
8. It drove Brian to hunt
9. Gift from Brian's mother
12. Brian's first food
14. The senseless attack of this animal drove Brian into the water
17. They helped Brian think of ways to survive
19. Plane crashed into it
20. Brian used a ___ and arrows to kill the rabbits
21. Plane started out in New ___
22. Brian's second food

Down
1. The ___ buyer rescued Brian
3. Where Brian stored his food after the skunk got the eggs
4. Brian unknowingly activated the emergency one
5. That Brian knew he could learn and survive was ___ Hope
7. It saw Brian near the berry bushes but did not attack
10. Number of hours Brian was blinded by the skunk
11. The ___ was that Brian saw his mother with another man
12. Where Brian was going
13. Mr. ___ worked in the oil fields in Canada
14. They made a living coat on Brian's skin
15. The ___ plane didn't see Brian and turned away
16. Model of the plane that crashed
18. Mall where Brian saw his mother and the other man

Hatchet Crossword 2 Answer Key

	1 F	I	R	E				2 P	3 I	L	O	T
	U								L			E
4 T	U	5 R	T	L	E			6 P	O	N	D	
R		O			7 B				G			
A		8 H	U	N	G	E	R		9 H	10 A	T	C	H	E	T
N		G			A	11 S				W		
S	12 C	H	13 E	R	R	I	E	S	14 M	O	15 O	S	E
M	A		R			C			O		E		16 C
I	N		B		17 D	R	18 E	A	M	S	19 L	A	K	E
T	A		E		E		M		Q		R		S
T	D		S		T		B		U		C		S
E	A	20 B	O	W			E		I		H		N
R			N				R		T				A
							21 Y	O	R	K		
									E			
	22 R	A	S	P	B	E	R	R	I	E	S	

Across
1. Friend that Brian created
2. He died of a heart attack
4. Brian took its eggs for food
6. Brian built one to store the fresh fish
8. It drove Brian to hunt
9. Gift from Brian's mother
12. Brian's first food
14. The senseless attack of this animal drove Brian into the water
17. They helped Brian think of ways to survive
19. Plane crashed into it
20. Brian used a ___ and arrows to kill the rabbits
21. Plane started out in New ___
22. Brian's second food

Down
1. The ___ buyer rescued Brian
3. Where Brian stored his food after the skunk got the eggs
4. Brian unknowingly activated the emergency one
5. That Brian knew he could learn and survive was ___ Hope
7. It saw Brian near the berry bushes but did not attack
10. Number of hours Brian was blinded by the skunk
11. The ___ was that Brian saw his mother with another man
12. Where Brian was going
13. Mr. ___ worked in the oil fields in Canada
14. They made a living coat on Brian's skin
15. The ___ plane didn't see Brian and turned away
16. Model of the plane that crashed
18. Mall where Brian saw his mother and the other man

Hatchet Crossword 3

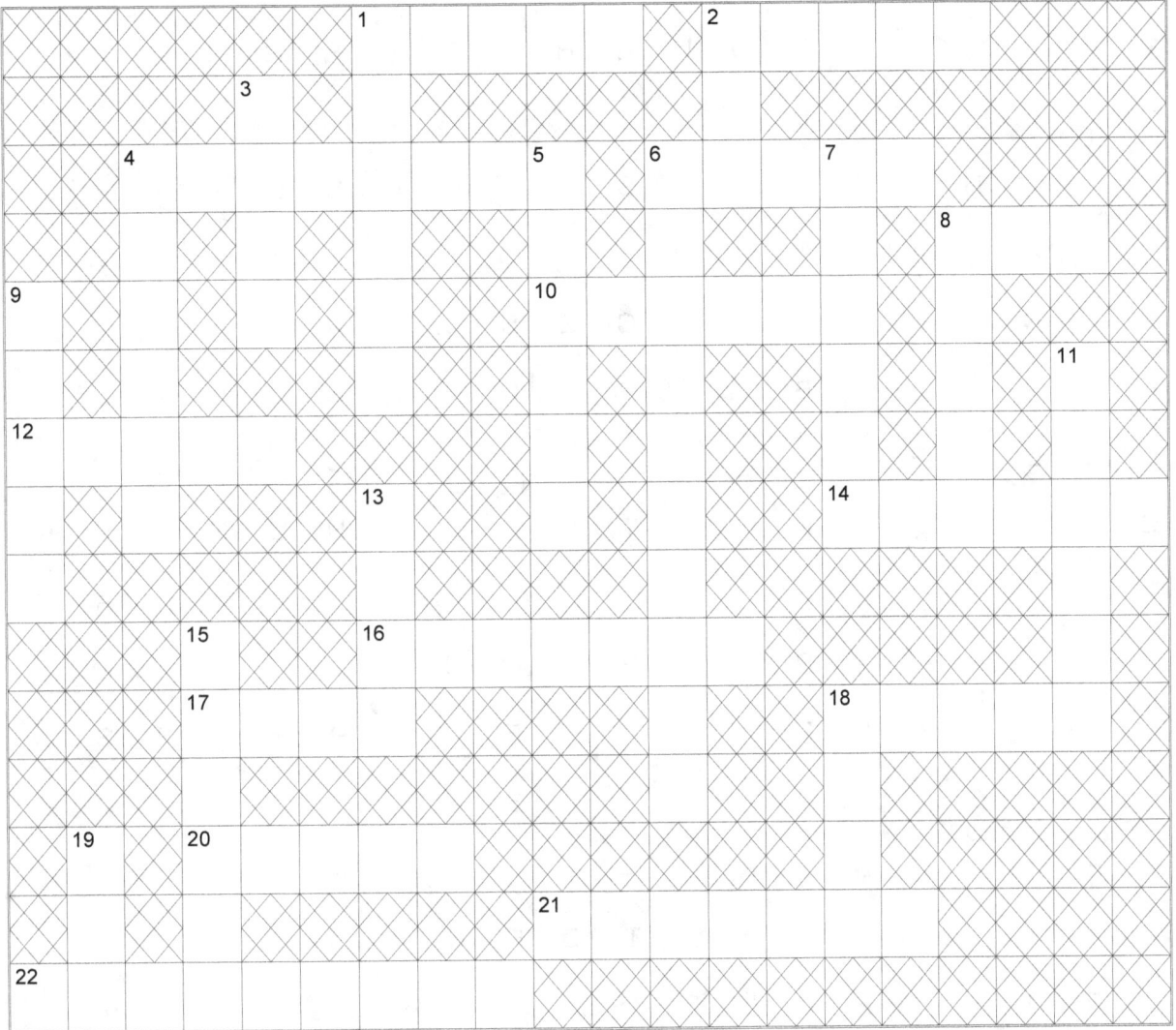

Across
1. That Brian knew he could learn and survive was ___ Hope
2. Pretended to be lost in the woods with Brian
4. Brian's first food
6. The senseless attack of this animal drove Brian into the water
8. Brian used a ___ and arrows to kill the rabbits
10. Model of the plane that crashed
12. Where Brian stored his food after the skunk got the eggs
14. It drove Brian to hunt
16. Mr. ___ worked in the oil fields in Canada
17. Plane crashed into it
18. Interested in Brian for a few months upon his return
20. Mall where Brian saw his mother and the other man
21. It destroyed Brian's shelter
22. Raft Brian built to get to the plane: ___ One

Down
1. Brian took its eggs for food
2. Number of hours Brian was blinded by the skunk
3. It saw Brian near the berry bushes but did not attack
4. Where Brian was going
5. The ___ was that Brian saw his mother with another man
6. They made a living coat on Brian's skin
7. The ___ plane didn't see Brian and turned away
8. Teenage wilderness survivor
9. He died of a heart attack
11. They helped Brian think of ways to survive
13. Friend that Brian created
15. The plane that rescued Brian had these
18. Brian built one to store the fresh fish
19. The ___ buyer rescued Brian

Hatchet Crossword 3 Answer Key

						¹T	O	U	G	H		²T	E	R	R	Y	
				³B		U						W					
			⁴C	H	E	R	R	I	E	⁵S		⁶M	O	O	⁷S	E	
			A			A				E		O			E		⁸B	O	W
⁹P			N			R				¹⁰C	E	S	S	N	A		R
I			A			L				R		Q			R		¹¹D
¹²L	E	D	G	E						E		U			¹⁴C		A	R
O			A			¹³F				T		I			H	U	N	G	E	R
T						I						T					A	
			¹⁵F		¹⁶R	O	B	E	S	O	N						M	
			¹⁷L	A	K	E				E				¹⁸P	R	E	S	S
			O							S				O			
	¹⁹F		²⁰A	M	B	E	R							N			
	U		T							²¹T	O	R	N	A	D	O	
²²B	R	U	S	H	P	I	L	E									

Across
1. That Brian knew he could learn and survive was ___ Hope
2. Pretended to be lost in the woods with Brian
4. Brian's first food
6. The senseless attack of this animal drove Brian into the water
8. Brian used a ___ and arrows to kill the rabbits
10. Model of the plane that crashed
12. Where Brian stored his food after the skunk got the eggs
14. It drove Brian to hunt
16. Mr. ___ worked in the oil fields in Canada
17. Plane crashed into it
18. Interested in Brian for a few months upon his return
20. Mall where Brian saw his mother and the other man
21. It destroyed Brian's shelter
22. Raft Brian built to get to the plane: ___ One

Down
1. Brian took its eggs for food
2. Number of hours Brian was blinded by the skunk
3. It saw Brian near the berry bushes but did not attack
4. Where Brian was going
5. The ___ was that Brian saw his mother with another man
6. They made a living coat on Brian's skin
7. The ___ plane didn't see Brian and turned away
8. Teenage wilderness survivor
9. He died of a heart attack
11. They helped Brian think of ways to survive
13. Friend that Brian created
15. The plane that rescued Brian had these
18. Brian built one to store the fresh fish
19. The ___ buyer rescued Brian

Hatchet Crossword 4

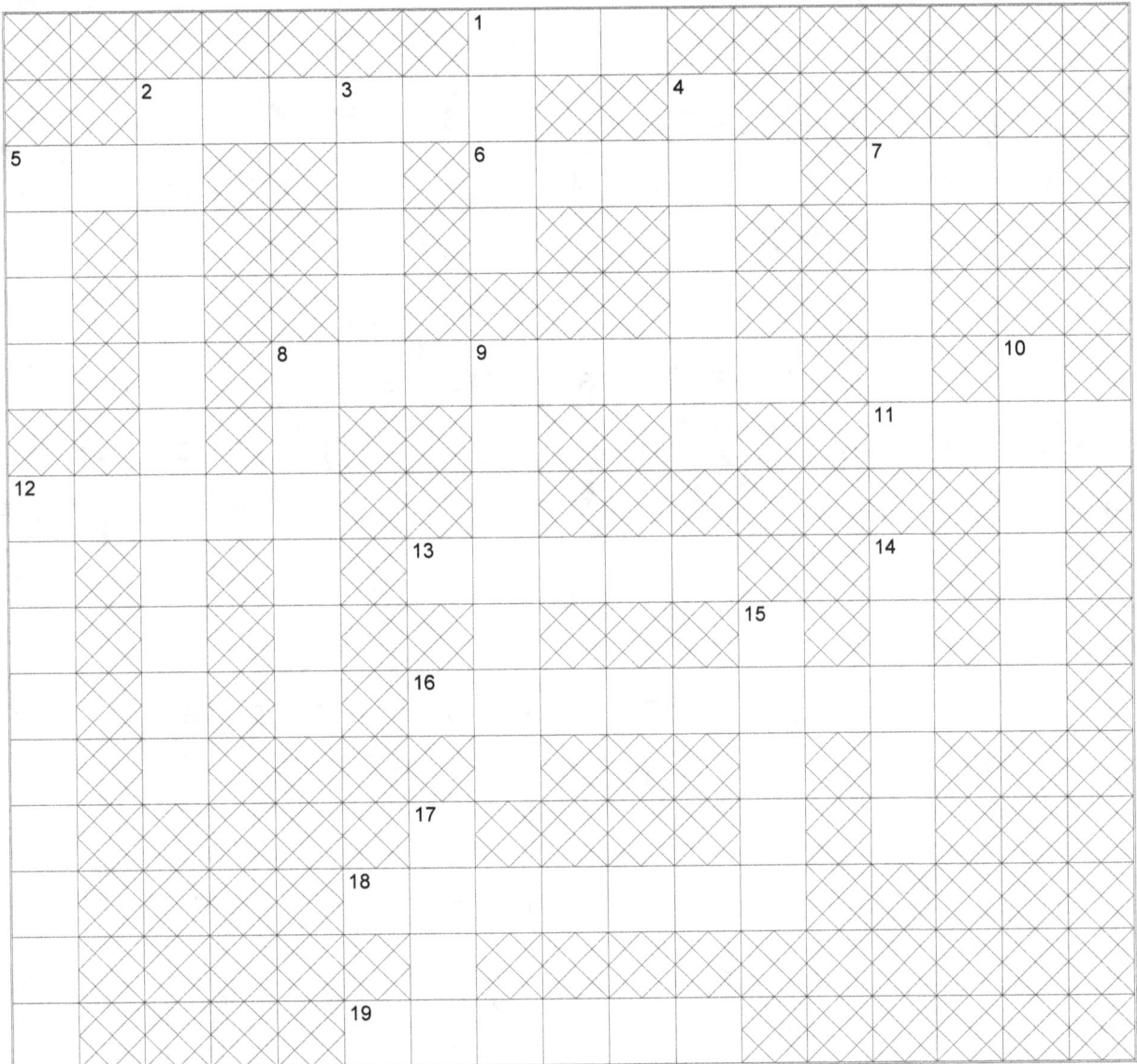

Across
1. Brian used a ___ and arrows to kill the rabbits
2. Brian took its eggs for food
5. The ___ buyer rescued Brian
6. Mall where Brian saw his mother and the other man
7. Number of hours Brian was blinded by the skunk
8. Brian's first food
11. Plane started out in New ___
12. Teenage wilderness survivor
13. Where Brian stored his food after the skunk got the eggs
16. They made a living coat on Brian's skin
18. Gift from Brian's mother
19. Model of the plane that crashed

Down
1. It saw Brian near the berry bushes but did not attack
2. Brian unknowingly activated the emergency one
3. That Brian knew he could learn and survive was ___ Hope
4. The ___ was that Brian saw his mother with another man
5. Friend that Brian created
7. Pretended to be lost in the woods with Brian
8. Where Brian was going
9. Mr. ___ worked in the oil fields in Canada
10. They helped Brian think of ways to survive
12. Raft Brian built to get to the plane: ___ One
14. The senseless attack of this animal drove Brian into the water
15. He died of a heart attack
17. Plane crashed into it

Hatchet Crossword 4 Answer Key

						1 B	O	W				
		2 T	U	R	3 T	L	E		4 S			
5 F	U	R			O		6 A	M	B	E	R	7 T	W	O
I		A			U		R		C			E
R		N			G		R					R
E		S		8 C	H	E	9 R	R	I	E	S	R		10 D
		M		A			O			T		11 Y	O	R	K
12 B	R	I	A	N			B							E
R		T		A		13 L	E	D	G	E		14 M		A
U		T		D		S				15 P		O		M
S		E		A		16 M	O	S	Q	U	I	T	O	E	S
H		R				O				L		S	
P						N				17 L		S	
I					18 H	A	T	C	H	E	T		
L						K				
E					19 C	E	S	S	N	A			

Across
1. Brian used a ___ and arrows to kill the rabbits
2. Brian took its eggs for food
5. The ___ buyer rescued Brian
6. Mall where Brian saw his mother and the other man
7. Number of hours Brian was blinded by the skunk
8. Brian's first food
11. Plane started out in New ___
12. Teenage wilderness survivor
13. Where Brian stored his food after the skunk got the eggs
16. They made a living coat on Brian's skin
18. Gift from Brian's mother
19. Model of the plane that crashed

Down
1. It saw Brian near the berry bushes but did not attack
2. Brian unknowingly activated the emergency one
3. That Brian knew he could learn and survive was ___ Hope
4. The ___ was that Brian saw his mother with another man
5. Friend that Brian created
7. Pretended to be lost in the woods with Brian
8. Where Brian was going
9. Mr. ___ worked in the oil fields in Canada
10. They helped Brian think of ways to survive
12. Raft Brian built to get to the plane: ___ One
14. The senseless attack of this animal drove Brian into the water
15. He died of a heart attack
17. Plane crashed into it

Hatchet

PERPICH	CANADA	FIRE	THIRTEEN	MOSQUITOES
TERRY	SECRET	FUR	BOW	ROBESON
FOOLBIRD	BRIAN	FREE SPACE	SURVIVAL	TURTLE
RASPBERRIES	TOUGH	MOOSE	CHERRIES	PAULSEN
DREAMS	LAKE	CESSNA	PORCUPINE	BEAR

Hatchet

PILOT	BRUSHPILE	LEDGE	FLOATS	DIVORCE
TWO	YORK	TRANSMITTER	POND	AMBER
SEARCH	HUNGER	FREE SPACE	PRESS	TORNADO
BEAR	PORCUPINE	CESSNA	LAKE	DREAMS
PAULSEN	CHERRIES	MOOSE	TOUGH	RASPBERRIES

Hatchet

CHERRIES	RASPBERRIES	LEDGE	BOW	PERPICH
DREAMS	TORNADO	FOOLBIRD	PRESS	AMBER
THIRTEEN	LAKE	FREE SPACE	BEAR	CANADA
BRIAN	FIFTYFOUR	TURTLE	DIVORCE	PILOT
TWO	FIRE	MOOSE	CESSNA	TERRY

Hatchet

SURVIVAL	BRUSHPILE	YORK	FLOATS	POND
SECRET	HATCHET	ROBESON	PORCUPINE	FUR
SEARCH	TRANSMITTER	FREE SPACE	TOUGH	PAULSEN
TERRY	CESSNA	MOOSE	FIRE	TWO
PILOT	DIVORCE	TURTLE	FIFTYFOUR	BRIAN

Hatchet

DIVORCE	DREAMS	SECRET	CHERRIES	TERRY
PAULSEN	CESSNA	THIRTEEN	PRESS	FLOATS
PERPICH	FIRE	FREE SPACE	TURTLE	SURVIVAL
ROBESON	HUNGER	BEAR	FUR	BRIAN
SEARCH	MOOSE	AMBER	FOOLBIRD	TRANSMITTER

Hatchet

CANADA	BOW	BRUSHPILE	HATCHET	LEDGE
YORK	TOUGH	TORNADO	PILOT	POND
RASPBERRIES	LAKE	FREE SPACE	TWO	MOSQUITOES
TRANSMITTER	FOOLBIRD	AMBER	MOOSE	SEARCH
BRIAN	FUR	BEAR	HUNGER	ROBESON

Hatchet

TURTLE	BEAR	TWO	CESSNA	DIVORCE
LEDGE	DREAMS	TERRY	AMBER	SECRET
BRIAN	THIRTEEN	FREE SPACE	FLOATS	CHERRIES
FIFTYFOUR	MOOSE	PILOT	POND	CANADA
LAKE	ROBESON	SEARCH	PAULSEN	HATCHET

Hatchet

FUR	FOOLBIRD	TOUGH	YORK	MOSQUITOES
SURVIVAL	BOW	RASPBERRIES	BRUSHPILE	TORNADO
PORCUPINE	PRESS	FREE SPACE	HUNGER	PERPICH
HATCHET	PAULSEN	SEARCH	ROBESON	LAKE
CANADA	POND	PILOT	MOOSE	FIFTYFOUR

Hatchet

AMBER	PILOT	SURVIVAL	BEAR	TERRY
CANADA	TURTLE	MOOSE	CHERRIES	FOOLBIRD
TRANSMITTER	HUNGER	FREE SPACE	FIFTYFOUR	PERPICH
MOSQUITOES	FUR	POND	PAULSEN	YORK
PRESS	CESSNA	RASPBERRIES	ROBESON	TORNADO

Hatchet

TOUGH	LAKE	DIVORCE	LEDGE	FLOATS
DREAMS	PORCUPINE	SEARCH	BRIAN	BOW
SECRET	FIRE	FREE SPACE	TWO	BRUSHPILE
TORNADO	ROBESON	RASPBERRIES	CESSNA	PRESS
YORK	PAULSEN	POND	FUR	MOSQUITOES

Hatchet

TORNADO	PORCUPINE	SEARCH	ROBESON	DIVORCE
TRANSMITTER	SECRET	TOUGH	BOW	PILOT
CHERRIES	THIRTEEN	FREE SPACE	PAULSEN	TURTLE
POND	MOSQUITOES	TERRY	BRIAN	LEDGE
HUNGER	TWO	SURVIVAL	YORK	RASPBERRIES

Hatchet

AMBER	BEAR	CESSNA	MOOSE	PERPICH
DREAMS	CANADA	FOOLBIRD	FUR	FLOATS
BRUSHPILE	LAKE	FREE SPACE	FIFTYFOUR	HATCHET
RASPBERRIES	YORK	SURVIVAL	TWO	HUNGER
LEDGE	BRIAN	TERRY	MOSQUITOES	POND

Hatchet

YORK	PORCUPINE	FIRE	CANADA	PRESS
TERRY	BOW	MOOSE	FIFTYFOUR	BRIAN
FOOLBIRD	DREAMS	FREE SPACE	AMBER	FLOATS
BEAR	HUNGER	MOSQUITOES	SEARCH	TRANSMITTER
DIVORCE	BRUSHPILE	RASPBERRIES	POND	TWO

Hatchet

PAULSEN	LEDGE	TURTLE	CHERRIES	HATCHET
PERPICH	SECRET	TOUGH	SURVIVAL	CESSNA
LAKE	THIRTEEN	FREE SPACE	FUR	TORNADO
TWO	POND	RASPBERRIES	BRUSHPILE	DIVORCE
TRANSMITTER	SEARCH	MOSQUITOES	HUNGER	BEAR

Hatchet

PILOT	CHERRIES	TOUGH	PAULSEN	FUR
SURVIVAL	SEARCH	MOOSE	HUNGER	RASPBERRIES
TORNADO	PRESS	FREE SPACE	HATCHET	YORK
DIVORCE	CESSNA	FOOLBIRD	THIRTEEN	BEAR
AMBER	TRANSMITTER	PERPICH	ROBESON	FLOATS

Hatchet

DREAMS	BOW	PORCUPINE	CANADA	SECRET
MOSQUITOES	POND	TERRY	LEDGE	TURTLE
TWO	FIRE	FREE SPACE	BRUSHPILE	LAKE
FLOATS	ROBESON	PERPICH	TRANSMITTER	AMBER
BEAR	THIRTEEN	FOOLBIRD	CESSNA	DIVORCE

Hatchet

MOSQUITOES	BRIAN	MOOSE	FLOATS	SEARCH
DREAMS	BOW	FIFTYFOUR	LEDGE	DIVORCE
SURVIVAL	BRUSHPILE	FREE SPACE	TURTLE	HATCHET
CHERRIES	BEAR	PERPICH	FIRE	AMBER
THIRTEEN	TOUGH	FOOLBIRD	PILOT	TORNADO

Hatchet

TRANSMITTER	RASPBERRIES	CANADA	YORK	PORCUPINE
SECRET	ROBESON	PRESS	TWO	POND
TERRY	FUR	FREE SPACE	LAKE	PAULSEN
TORNADO	PILOT	FOOLBIRD	TOUGH	THIRTEEN
AMBER	FIRE	PERPICH	BEAR	CHERRIES

Hatchet

RASPBERRIES	MOSQUITOES	SURVIVAL	PRESS	TWO
FUR	YORK	PORCUPINE	TORNADO	BRUSHPILE
BEAR	BRIAN	FREE SPACE	CESSNA	BOW
ROBESON	POND	FLOATS	FIFTYFOUR	FIRE
MOOSE	PERPICH	DREAMS	LEDGE	DIVORCE

Hatchet

HATCHET	LAKE	TURTLE	CANADA	PAULSEN
TERRY	PILOT	FOOLBIRD	SEARCH	TOUGH
THIRTEEN	SECRET	FREE SPACE	CHERRIES	AMBER
DIVORCE	LEDGE	DREAMS	PERPICH	MOOSE
FIRE	FIFTYFOUR	FLOATS	POND	ROBESON

Hatchet

FIRE	THIRTEEN	BOW	TOUGH	SURVIVAL
MOSQUITOES	SEARCH	HATCHET	PERPICH	AMBER
BRUSHPILE	ROBESON	FREE SPACE	TORNADO	DREAMS
PRESS	TWO	PILOT	YORK	BRIAN
PAULSEN	FLOATS	LEDGE	FOOLBIRD	BEAR

Hatchet

LAKE	CANADA	CESSNA	DIVORCE	TURTLE
MOOSE	FUR	TERRY	PORCUPINE	HUNGER
POND	CHERRIES	FREE SPACE	TRANSMITTER	RASPBERRIES
BEAR	FOOLBIRD	LEDGE	FLOATS	PAULSEN
BRIAN	YORK	PILOT	TWO	PRESS

Hatchet

LEDGE	MOOSE	SURVIVAL	SECRET	FOOLBIRD
SEARCH	TWO	PORCUPINE	BRUSHPILE	RASPBERRIES
HATCHET	TERRY	FREE SPACE	PERPICH	DIVORCE
PRESS	TOUGH	FIFTYFOUR	TRANSMITTER	PILOT
LAKE	CESSNA	BOW	THIRTEEN	HUNGER

Hatchet

YORK	DREAMS	FIRE	FLOATS	FUR
BRIAN	ROBESON	TORNADO	CANADA	AMBER
PAULSEN	BEAR	FREE SPACE	TURTLE	POND
HUNGER	THIRTEEN	BOW	CESSNA	LAKE
PILOT	TRANSMITTER	FIFTYFOUR	TOUGH	PRESS

Hatchet

SEARCH	THIRTEEN	TORNADO	LAKE	HUNGER
FLOATS	YORK	DREAMS	PILOT	CHERRIES
FOOLBIRD	TWO	FREE SPACE	BRIAN	TOUGH
BEAR	POND	PERPICH	FUR	MOSQUITOES
RASPBERRIES	TERRY	CESSNA	FIRE	PORCUPINE

Hatchet

HATCHET	PRESS	MOOSE	AMBER	SECRET
CANADA	BOW	TURTLE	LEDGE	SURVIVAL
TRANSMITTER	BRUSHPILE	FREE SPACE	FIFTYFOUR	PAULSEN
PORCUPINE	FIRE	CESSNA	TERRY	RASPBERRIES
MOSQUITOES	FUR	PERPICH	POND	BEAR

Hatchet

BEAR	YORK	TORNADO	PAULSEN	HATCHET
TOUGH	THIRTEEN	PERPICH	TERRY	FIRE
TWO	FLOATS	FREE SPACE	MOSQUITOES	LEDGE
BOW	BRIAN	CHERRIES	ROBESON	TURTLE
FUR	PORCUPINE	SEARCH	FIFTYFOUR	CESSNA

Hatchet

AMBER	LAKE	TRANSMITTER	DREAMS	BRUSHPILE
DIVORCE	SECRET	FOOLBIRD	SURVIVAL	RASPBERRIES
CANADA	MOOSE	FREE SPACE	HUNGER	PILOT
CESSNA	FIFTYFOUR	SEARCH	PORCUPINE	FUR
TURTLE	ROBESON	CHERRIES	BRIAN	BOW

Hatchet

PILOT	FUR	DREAMS	LAKE	SECRET
FIRE	FIFTYFOUR	FLOATS	TORNADO	CANADA
ROBESON	TERRY	FREE SPACE	TURTLE	FOOLBIRD
TRANSMITTER	CESSNA	DIVORCE	TOUGH	SEARCH
MOOSE	MOSQUITOES	BEAR	CHERRIES	BOW

Hatchet

POND	AMBER	PERPICH	HATCHET	LEDGE
YORK	PRESS	BRIAN	BRUSHPILE	PORCUPINE
THIRTEEN	RASPBERRIES	FREE SPACE	HUNGER	PAULSEN
BOW	CHERRIES	BEAR	MOSQUITOES	MOOSE
SEARCH	TOUGH	DIVORCE	CESSNA	TRANSMITTER

Hatchet

FIFTYFOUR	PRESS	ROBESON	HUNGER	PILOT
TORNADO	TWO	SEARCH	AMBER	FUR
FOOLBIRD	HATCHET	FREE SPACE	CANADA	LEDGE
THIRTEEN	MOSQUITOES	DREAMS	BEAR	SURVIVAL
FIRE	PERPICH	TURTLE	TRANSMITTER	BRUSHPILE

Hatchet

PAULSEN	CESSNA	LAKE	POND	BRIAN
YORK	DIVORCE	MOOSE	TERRY	CHERRIES
RASPBERRIES	PORCUPINE	FREE SPACE	SECRET	FLOATS
BRUSHPILE	TRANSMITTER	TURTLE	PERPICH	FIRE
SURVIVAL	BEAR	DREAMS	MOSQUITOES	THIRTEEN

Hatchet Vocabulary Word List

No.	Word	Clue/Definition
1.	ABATED	Lessened; diminished
2.	ACCURATELY	Correctly
3.	ANTISEPTIC	Disinfectant; kills germs
4.	ASSET	Advantage; resource
5.	CRUDE	Rough
6.	DRONE	A continuous humming sound
7.	EXASPERATION	Annoyance
8.	EXULTED	Rejoiced
9.	FLAILING	Waving or swinging vigorously
10.	FUROR	Intense excitement
11.	GORGE	Stuff; devour
12.	GRIMACING	Twisting the face to show pain
13.	HEFTED	Lifted; heaved
14.	INFURIATING	Aggravating; maddening
15.	INSTINCTIVE	Natural; intuitive
16.	KEENING	Piercing; intense
17.	LUNGED	Dashed; charged
18.	MASSIVELY	Enormously
19.	PERSISTENT	Enduring; not giving up
20.	PRECIOUS	Valuable
21.	PRONG	Thin, pointed, projecting part
22.	PULVERIZED	Ground up; crumbled
23.	RECEDED	Withdrew; went back
24.	RUEFULLY	Regretfully
25.	SEEPING	Dripping; trickling
26.	SEGMENT	Section; part
27.	SPASM	Involuntary muscle contraction
28.	SPIRALING	Twisting; winding
29.	STABLE	Steady; firm
30.	STAGGERING	Overwhelming
31.	STYMIED	Stumped; stuck in puzzlement
32.	TENDRILS	Long, slender, curling strands
33.	TRANSMITTER	An electronic device that sends a signal
34.	UNDULY	Excessively
35.	UNWITTINGLY	Not knowing; not intended
36.	WALLOW	Roll around
37.	WRENCHING	Tearing; turning; twisting

Hatchet Vocabulary Fill In The Blank 1

_____ 1. Involuntary muscle contraction

_____ 2. Intense excitement

_____ 3. Piercing; intense

_____ 4. Lifted; heaved

_____ 5. Regretfully

_____ 6. Lessened; diminished

_____ 7. Thin, pointed, projecting part

_____ 8. Natural; intuitive

_____ 9. Not knowing; not intended

_____ 10. Ground up; crumbled

_____ 11. Twisting; winding

_____ 12. Rough

_____ 13. Twisting the face to show pain

_____ 14. An electronic device that sends a signal

_____ 15. Annoyance

_____ 16. Long, slender, curling strands

_____ 17. Enormously

_____ 18. Disinfectant; kills germs

_____ 19. Dripping; trickling

_____ 20. Withdrew; went back

Hatchet Vocabulary Fill In The Blank 1 Answer Key

SPASM	1. Involuntary muscle contraction
FUROR	2. Intense excitement
KEENING	3. Piercing; intense
HEFTED	4. Lifted; heaved
RUEFULLY	5. Regretfully
ABATED	6. Lessened; diminished
PRONG	7. Thin, pointed, projecting part
INSTINCTIVE	8. Natural; intuitive
UNWITTINGLY	9. Not knowing; not intended
PULVERIZED	10. Ground up; crumbled
SPIRALING	11. Twisting; winding
CRUDE	12. Rough
GRIMACING	13. Twisting the face to show pain
TRANSMITTER	14. An electronic device that sends a signal
EXASPERATION	15. Annoyance
TENDRILS	16. Long, slender, curling strands
MASSIVELY	17. Enormously
ANTISEPTIC	18. Disinfectant; kills germs
SEEPING	19. Dripping; trickling
RECEDED	20. Withdrew; went back

Hatchet Vocabulary Fill In The Blank 2

_____ 1. A continuous humming sound

_____ 2. Enormously

_____ 3. Natural; intuitive

_____ 4. Steady; firm

_____ 5. Valuable

_____ 6. Stumped; stuck in puzzlement

_____ 7. Withdrew; went back

_____ 8. Twisting; winding

_____ 9. Stuff; devour

_____ 10. Section; part

_____ 11. Long, slender, curling strands

_____ 12. Ground up; crumbled

_____ 13. Regretfully

_____ 14. Dashed; charged

_____ 15. Dripping; trickling

_____ 16. Lessened; diminished

_____ 17. Rejoiced

_____ 18. Aggravating; maddening

_____ 19. Annoyance

_____ 20. Rough

Hatchet Vocabulary Fill In The Blank 2 Answer Key

DRONE	1. A continuous humming sound
MASSIVELY	2. Enormously
INSTINCTIVE	3. Natural; intuitive
STABLE	4. Steady; firm
PRECIOUS	5. Valuable
STYMIED	6. Stumped; stuck in puzzlement
RECEDED	7. Withdrew; went back
SPIRALING	8. Twisting; winding
GORGE	9. Stuff; devour
SEGMENT	10. Section; part
TENDRILS	11. Long, slender, curling strands
PULVERIZED	12. Ground up; crumbled
RUEFULLY	13. Regretfully
LUNGED	14. Dashed; charged
SEEPING	15. Dripping; trickling
ABATED	16. Lessened; diminished
EXULTED	17. Rejoiced
INFURIATING	18. Aggravating; maddening
EXASPERATION	19. Annoyance
CRUDE	20. Rough

Hatchet Vocabulary Fill In The Blank 3

1. Annoyance
2. Dashed; charged
3. Steady; firm
4. Piercing; intense
5. Section; part
6. Withdrew; went back
7. Disinfectant; kills germs
8. Twisting; winding
9. Dripping; trickling
10. Not knowing; not intended
11. Stumped; stuck in puzzlement
12. A continuous humming sound
13. Long, slender, curling strands
14. Waving or swinging vigorously
15. Correctly
16. An electronic device that sends a signal
17. Ground up; crumbled
18. Roll around
19. Rough
20. Regretfully

Hatchet Vocabulary Fill In The Blank 3 Answer Key

EXASPERATION	1. Annoyance
LUNGED	2. Dashed; charged
STABLE	3. Steady; firm
KEENING	4. Piercing; intense
SEGMENT	5. Section; part
RECEDED	6. Withdrew; went back
ANTISEPTIC	7. Disinfectant; kills germs
SPIRALING	8. Twisting; winding
SEEPING	9. Dripping; trickling
UNWITTINGLY	10. Not knowing; not intended
STYMIED	11. Stumped; stuck in puzzlement
DRONE	12. A continuous humming sound
TENDRILS	13. Long, slender, curling strands
FLAILING	14. Waving or swinging vigorously
ACCURATELY	15. Correctly
TRANSMITTER	16. An electronic device that sends a signal
PULVERIZED	17. Ground up; crumbled
WALLOW	18. Roll around
CRUDE	19. Rough
RUEFULLY	20. Regretfully

Hatchet Vocabulary Fill In The Blank 4

_____ 1. Rejoiced

_____ 2. Valuable

_____ 3. Waving or swinging vigorously

_____ 4. Rough

_____ 5. Lifted; heaved

_____ 6. Natural; intuitive

_____ 7. Intense excitement

_____ 8. Ground up; crumbled

_____ 9. An electronic device that sends a signal

_____ 10. Correctly

_____ 11. Aggravating; maddening

_____ 12. Disinfectant; kills germs

_____ 13. Stumped; stuck in puzzlement

_____ 14. Dripping; trickling

_____ 15. Long, slender, curling strands

_____ 16. Thin, pointed, projecting part

_____ 17. Enduring; not giving up

_____ 18. Steady; firm

_____ 19. Piercing; intense

_____ 20. Regretfully

Hatchet Vocabulary Fill In The Blank 4 Answer Key

EXULTED	1. Rejoiced
PRECIOUS	2. Valuable
FLAILING	3. Waving or swinging vigorously
CRUDE	4. Rough
HEFTED	5. Lifted; heaved
INSTINCTIVE	6. Natural; intuitive
FUROR	7. Intense excitement
PULVERIZED	8. Ground up; crumbled
TRANSMITTER	9. An electronic device that sends a signal
ACCURATELY	10. Correctly
INFURIATING	11. Aggravating; maddening
ANTISEPTIC	12. Disinfectant; kills germs
STYMIED	13. Stumped; stuck in puzzlement
SEEPING	14. Dripping; trickling
TENDRILS	15. Long, slender, curling strands
PRONG	16. Thin, pointed, projecting part
PERSISTENT	17. Enduring; not giving up
STABLE	18. Steady; firm
KEENING	19. Piercing; intense
RUEFULLY	20. Regretfully

Hatchet Vocabulary Matching 1

___ 1. TENDRILS   A. Enormously
___ 2. UNDULY   B. Overwhelming
___ 3. DRONE   C. Stuff; devour
___ 4. SEEPING   D. Excessively
___ 5. TRANSMITTER   E. Regretfully
___ 6. WRENCHING   F. Advantage; resource
___ 7. SEGMENT   G. Not knowing; not intended
___ 8. PERSISTENT   H. A continuous humming sound
___ 9. PULVERIZED   I. Ground up; crumbled
___10. SPASM   J. Twisting the face to show pain
___11. ANTISEPTIC   K. Dripping; trickling
___12. RUEFULLY   L. Dashed; charged
___13. GORGE   M. Disinfectant; kills germs
___14. STAGGERING   N. Waving or swinging vigorously
___15. KEENING   O. Natural; intuitive
___16. ASSET   P. Steady; firm
___17. MASSIVELY   Q. Involuntary muscle contraction
___18. FLAILING   R. Section; part
___19. INSTINCTIVE   S. Long, slender, curling strands
___20. FUROR   T. Tearing; turning; twisting
___21. SPIRALING   U. Intense excitement
___22. UNWITTINGLY   V. Enduring; not giving up
___23. GRIMACING   W. An electronic device that sends a signal
___24. STABLE   X. Piercing; intense
___25. LUNGED   Y. Twisting; winding

Hatchet Vocabulary Matching 1 Answer Key

S - 1. TENDRILS	A.	Enormously
D - 2. UNDULY	B.	Overwhelming
H - 3. DRONE	C.	Stuff; devour
K - 4. SEEPING	D.	Excessively
W - 5. TRANSMITTER	E.	Regretfully
T - 6. WRENCHING	F.	Advantage; resource
R - 7. SEGMENT	G.	Not knowing; not intended
V - 8. PERSISTENT	H.	A continuous humming sound
I - 9. PULVERIZED	I.	Ground up; crumbled
Q - 10. SPASM	J.	Twisting the face to show pain
M - 11. ANTISEPTIC	K.	Dripping; trickling
E - 12. RUEFULLY	L.	Dashed; charged
C - 13. GORGE	M.	Disinfectant; kills germs
B - 14. STAGGERING	N.	Waving or swinging vigorously
X - 15. KEENING	O.	Natural; intuitive
F - 16. ASSET	P.	Steady; firm
A - 17. MASSIVELY	Q.	Involuntary muscle contraction
N - 18. FLAILING	R.	Section; part
O - 19. INSTINCTIVE	S.	Long, slender, curling strands
U - 20. FUROR	T.	Tearing; turning; twisting
Y - 21. SPIRALING	U.	Intense excitement
G - 22. UNWITTINGLY	V.	Enduring; not giving up
J - 23. GRIMACING	W.	An electronic device that sends a signal
P - 24. STABLE	X.	Piercing; intense
L - 25. LUNGED	Y.	Twisting; winding

Hatchet Vocabulary Matching 2

___ 1. ASSET   A. Tearing; turning; twisting
___ 2. SPASM   B. Long, slender, curling strands
___ 3. PRONG   C. Involuntary muscle contraction
___ 4. ACCURATELY   D. An electronic device that sends a signal
___ 5. TENDRILS   E. Correctly
___ 6. PERSISTENT   F. Piercing; intense
___ 7. STAGGERING   G. Lifted; heaved
___ 8. GRIMACING   H. Dripping; trickling
___ 9. FLAILING   I. Dashed; charged
___10. SEEPING   J. Advantage; resource
___11. STYMIED   K. Twisting; winding
___12. ABATED   L. Twisting the face to show pain
___13. WRENCHING   M. Disinfectant; kills germs
___14. INFURIATING   N. Aggravating; maddening
___15. EXASPERATION   O. Stuff; devour
___16. HEFTED   P. Stumped; stuck in puzzlement
___17. GORGE   Q. Waving or swinging vigorously
___18. LUNGED   R. Overwhelming
___19. TRANSMITTER   S. Thin, pointed, projecting part
___20. ANTISEPTIC   T. Steady; firm
___21. KEENING   U. Enormously
___22. MASSIVELY   V. Annoyance
___23. EXULTED   W. Rejoiced
___24. STABLE   X. Enduring; not giving up
___25. SPIRALING   Y. Lessened; diminished

Hatchet Vocabulary Matching 2 Answer Key

J - 1.	ASSET	A. Tearing; turning; twisting
C - 2.	SPASM	B. Long, slender, curling strands
S - 3.	PRONG	C. Involuntary muscle contraction
E - 4.	ACCURATELY	D. An electronic device that sends a signal
B - 5.	TENDRILS	E. Correctly
X - 6.	PERSISTENT	F. Piercing; intense
R - 7.	STAGGERING	G. Lifted; heaved
L - 8.	GRIMACING	H. Dripping; trickling
Q - 9.	FLAILING	I. Dashed; charged
H - 10.	SEEPING	J. Advantage; resource
P - 11.	STYMIED	K. Twisting; winding
Y - 12.	ABATED	L. Twisting the face to show pain
A - 13.	WRENCHING	M. Disinfectant; kills germs
N - 14.	INFURIATING	N. Aggravating; maddening
V - 15.	EXASPERATION	O. Stuff; devour
G - 16.	HEFTED	P. Stumped; stuck in puzzlement
O - 17.	GORGE	Q. Waving or swinging vigorously
I - 18.	LUNGED	R. Overwhelming
D - 19.	TRANSMITTER	S. Thin, pointed, projecting part
M - 20.	ANTISEPTIC	T. Steady; firm
F - 21.	KEENING	U. Enormously
U - 22.	MASSIVELY	V. Annoyance
W - 23.	EXULTED	W. Rejoiced
T - 24.	STABLE	X. Enduring; not giving up
K - 25.	SPIRALING	Y. Lessened; diminished

Hatchet Vocabulary Matching 3

___ 1. GORGE   A. Disinfectant; kills germs
___ 2. UNDULY   B. Tearing; turning; twisting
___ 3. TENDRILS   C. Piercing; intense
___ 4. MASSIVELY   D. Valuable
___ 5. UNWITTINGLY   E. Excessively
___ 6. TRANSMITTER   F. Enormously
___ 7. ASSET   G. Twisting; winding
___ 8. FUROR   H. Waving or swinging vigorously
___ 9. SPIRALING   I. Roll around
___10. STABLE   J. Advantage; resource
___11. WRENCHING   K. Stuff; devour
___12. FLAILING   L. Stumped; stuck in puzzlement
___13. EXASPERATION M. Overwhelming
___14. INFURIATING   N. An electronic device that sends a signal
___15. PRONG   O. Intense excitement
___16. STYMIED   P. Aggravating; maddening
___17. RECEDED   Q. Annoyance
___18. SEEPING   R. Steady; firm
___19. ABATED   S. Thin, pointed, projecting part
___20. KEENING   T. Long, slender, curling strands
___21. STAGGERING   U. Withdrew; went back
___22. WALLOW   V. Rough
___23. ANTISEPTIC   W. Dripping; trickling
___24. PRECIOUS   X. Not knowing; not intended
___25. CRUDE   Y. Lessened; diminished

Hatchet Vocabulary Matching 3 Answer Key

K - 1.	GORGE	A.	Disinfectant; kills germs
E - 2.	UNDULY	B.	Tearing; turning; twisting
T - 3.	TENDRILS	C.	Piercing; intense
F - 4.	MASSIVELY	D.	Valuable
X - 5.	UNWITTINGLY	E.	Excessively
N - 6.	TRANSMITTER	F.	Enormously
J - 7.	ASSET	G.	Twisting; winding
O - 8.	FUROR	H.	Waving or swinging vigorously
G - 9.	SPIRALING	I.	Roll around
R - 10.	STABLE	J.	Advantage; resource
B - 11.	WRENCHING	K.	Stuff; devour
H - 12.	FLAILING	L.	Stumped; stuck in puzzlement
Q - 13.	EXASPERATION	M.	Overwhelming
P - 14.	INFURIATING	N.	An electronic device that sends a signal
S - 15.	PRONG	O.	Intense excitement
L - 16.	STYMIED	P.	Aggravating; maddening
U - 17.	RECEDED	Q.	Annoyance
W - 18.	SEEPING	R.	Steady; firm
Y - 19.	ABATED	S.	Thin, pointed, projecting part
C - 20.	KEENING	T.	Long, slender, curling strands
M - 21.	STAGGERING	U.	Withdrew; went back
I - 22.	WALLOW	V.	Rough
A - 23.	ANTISEPTIC	W.	Dripping; trickling
D - 24.	PRECIOUS	X.	Not knowing; not intended
V - 25.	CRUDE	Y.	Lessened; diminished

Hatchet Vocabulary Matching 4

___ 1. INFURIATING   A. Natural; intuitive
___ 2. SPIRALING   B. Rough
___ 3. PULVERIZED   C. A continuous humming sound
___ 4. LUNGED   D. Twisting; winding
___ 5. SPASM   E. Involuntary muscle contraction
___ 6. FUROR   F. An electronic device that sends a signal
___ 7. EXULTED   G. Piercing; intense
___ 8. PRONG   H. Tearing; turning; twisting
___ 9. SEEPING   I. Thin, pointed, projecting part
___10. INSTINCTIVE   J. Stumped; stuck in puzzlement
___11. UNDULY   K. Aggravating; maddening
___12. PERSISTENT   L. Ground up; crumbled
___13. DRONE   M. Enormously
___14. UNWITTINGLY   N. Enduring; not giving up
___15. RECEDED   O. Dashed; charged
___16. WALLOW   P. Advantage; resource
___17. CRUDE   Q. Rejoiced
___18. MASSIVELY   R. Not knowing; not intended
___19. KEENING   S. Roll around
___20. STYMIED   T. Withdrew; went back
___21. TRANSMITTER   U. Dripping; trickling
___22. STAGGERING   V. Intense excitement
___23. ASSET   W. Steady; firm
___24. WRENCHING   X. Overwhelming
___25. STABLE   Y. Excessively

Hatchet Vocabulary Matching 4 Answer Key

K - 1. INFURIATING	A.	Natural; intuitive
D - 2. SPIRALING	B.	Rough
L - 3. PULVERIZED	C.	A continuous humming sound
O - 4. LUNGED	D.	Twisting; winding
E - 5. SPASM	E.	Involuntary muscle contraction
V - 6. FUROR	F.	An electronic device that sends a signal
Q - 7. EXULTED	G.	Piercing; intense
I - 8. PRONG	H.	Tearing; turning; twisting
U - 9. SEEPING	I.	Thin, pointed, projecting part
A - 10. INSTINCTIVE	J.	Stumped; stuck in puzzlement
Y - 11. UNDULY	K.	Aggravating; maddening
N - 12. PERSISTENT	L.	Ground up; crumbled
C - 13. DRONE	M.	Enormously
R - 14. UNWITTINGLY	N.	Enduring; not giving up
T - 15. RECEDED	O.	Dashed; charged
S - 16. WALLOW	P.	Advantage; resource
B - 17. CRUDE	Q.	Rejoiced
M - 18. MASSIVELY	R.	Not knowing; not intended
G - 19. KEENING	S.	Roll around
J - 20. STYMIED	T.	Withdrew; went back
F - 21. TRANSMITTER	U.	Dripping; trickling
X - 22. STAGGERING	V.	Intense excitement
P - 23. ASSET	W.	Steady; firm
H - 24. WRENCHING	X.	Overwhelming
W - 25. STABLE	Y.	Excessively

Hatchet Vocabulary Magic Squares 1

A. SEGMENT	E. SPIRALING	I. CRUDE	M. WRENCHING
B. LUNGED	F. PRONG	J. GRIMACING	N. STABLE
C. UNDULY	G. STAGGERING	K. INFURIATING	O. SPASM
D. RECEDED	H. PRECIOUS	L. RUEFULLY	P. PERSISTENT

1. Tearing; turning; twisting
2. Thin, pointed, projecting part
3. Valuable
4. Involuntary muscle contraction
5. Regretfully
6. Excessively
7. Section; part
8. Twisting the face to show pain
9. Aggravating; maddening
10. Withdrew; went back
11. Dashed; charged
12. Rough
13. Steady; firm
14. Twisting; winding
15. Overwhelming
16. Enduring; not giving up

A=	B=	C=	D=
E=	F=	G=	H=
I=	J=	K=	L=
M=	N=	O=	P=

Hatchet Vocabulary Magic Squares 1 Answer Key

A. SEGMENT   E. SPIRALING   I. CRUDE   M. WRENCHING
B. LUNGED   F. PRONG   J. GRIMACING   N. STABLE
C. UNDULY   G. STAGGERING   K. INFURIATING   O. SPASM
D. RECEDED   H. PRECIOUS   L. RUEFULLY   P. PERSISTENT

1. Tearing; turning; twisting
2. Thin, pointed, projecting part
3. Valuable
4. Involuntary muscle contraction
5. Regretfully
6. Excessively
7. Section; part
8. Twisting the face to show pain
9. Aggravating; maddening
10. Withdrew; went back
11. Dashed; charged
12. Rough
13. Steady; firm
14. Twisting; winding
15. Overwhelming
16. Enduring; not giving up

A=7	B=11	C=6	D=10
E=14	F=2	G=15	H=3
I=12	J=8	K=9	L=5
M=1	N=13	O=4	P=16

Hatchet Vocabulary Magic Squares 2

A. CRUDE   E. WRENCHING   I. STYMIED   M. INSTINCTIVE
B. STAGGERING   F. EXASPERATION   J. SEEPING   N. DRONE
C. TRANSMITTER G. ACCURATELY   K. MASSIVELY   O. HEFTED
D. RUEFULLY   H. UNDULY   L. PULVERIZED   P. GORGE

1. Annoyance
2. Stumped; stuck in puzzlement
3. Lifted; heaved
4. Regretfully
5. Natural; intuitive
6. Overwhelming
7. Excessively
8. Enormously

9. An electronic device that sends a signal
10. Stuff; devour
11. Dripping; trickling
12. Tearing; turning; twisting
13. Ground up; crumbled
14. Correctly
15. Rough
16. A continuous humming sound

A=	B=	C=	D=
E=	F=	G=	H=
I=	J=	K=	L=
M=	N=	O=	P=

Hatchet Vocabulary Magic Squares 2 Answer Key

A. CRUDE
B. STAGGERING
C. TRANSMITTER
D. RUEFULLY
E. WRENCHING
F. EXASPERATION
G. ACCURATELY
H. UNDULY
I. STYMIED
J. SEEPING
K. MASSIVELY
L. PULVERIZED
M. INSTINCTIVE
N. DRONE
O. HEFTED
P. GORGE

1. Annoyance
2. Stumped; stuck in puzzlement
3. Lifted; heaved
4. Regretfully
5. Natural; intuitive
6. Overwhelming
7. Excessively
8. Enormously
9. An electronic device that sends a signal
10. Stuff; devour
11. Dripping; trickling
12. Tearing; turning; twisting
13. Ground up; crumbled
14. Correctly
15. Rough
16. A continuous humming sound

A=15	B=6	C=9	D=4
E=12	F=1	G=14	H=7
I=2	J=11	K=8	L=13
M=5	N=16	O=3	P=10

Hatchet Vocabulary Magic Squares 3

A. ABATED   E. PERSISTENT   I. KEENING   M. INFURIATING
B. UNWITTINGLY F. HEFTED   J. FLAILING   N. ACCURATELY
C. PRECIOUS   G. EXULTED   K. LUNGED   O. RUEFULLY
D. INSTINCTIVE H. FUROR   L. SEEPING   P. CRUDE

1. Correctly
2. Rejoiced
3. Dripping; trickling
4. Lessened; diminished
5. Dashed; charged
6. Not knowing; not intended
7. Aggravating; maddening
8. Intense excitement
9. Enduring; not giving up
10. Rough
11. Valuable
12. Waving or swinging vigorously
13. Natural; intuitive
14. Piercing; intense
15. Lifted; heaved
16. Regretfully

A=	B=	C=	D=
E=	F=	G=	H=
I=	J=	K=	L=
M=	N=	O=	P=

Hatchet Vocabulary Magic Squares 3 Answer Key

A. ABATED   E. PERSISTENT   I. KEENING   M. INFURIATING
B. UNWITTINGLY F. HEFTED   J. FLAILING   N. ACCURATELY
C. PRECIOUS   G. EXULTED   K. LUNGED   O. RUEFULLY
D. INSTINCTIVE H. FUROR   L. SEEPING   P. CRUDE

1. Correctly
2. Rejoiced
3. Dripping; trickling
4. Lessened; diminished
5. Dashed; charged
6. Not knowing; not intended
7. Aggravating; maddening
8. Intense excitement
9. Enduring; not giving up
10. Rough
11. Valuable
12. Waving or swinging vigorously
13. Natural; intuitive
14. Piercing; intense
15. Lifted; heaved
16. Regretfully

A=4	B=6	C=11	D=13
E=9	F=15	G=2	H=8
I=14	J=12	K=5	L=3
M=7	N=1	O=16	P=10

Hatchet Vocabulary Magic Squares 4

A. RECEDED
B. STAGGERING
C. TRANSMITTER
D. ABATED
E. ASSET
F. INFURIATING
G. GORGE
H. KEENING
I. DRONE
J. GRIMACING
K. HEFTED
L. TENDRILS
M. LUNGED
N. FUROR
O. EXULTED
P. STABLE

1. Withdrew; went back
2. Intense excitement
3. Twisting the face to show pain
4. Advantage; resource
5. Stuff; devour
6. Long, slender, curling strands
7. Steady; firm
8. An electronic device that sends a signal
9. Rejoiced
10. Lessened; diminished
11. Piercing; intense
12. Lifted; heaved
13. A continuous humming sound
14. Aggravating; maddening
15. Overwhelming
16. Dashed; charged

A=	B=	C=	D=
E=	F=	G=	H=
I=	J=	K=	L=
M=	N=	O=	P=

Hatchet Vocabulary Magic Squares 4 Answer Key

A. RECEDED	E. ASSET	I. DRONE	M. LUNGED
B. STAGGERING	F. INFURIATING	J. GRIMACING	N. FUROR
C. TRANSMITTER	G. GORGE	K. HEFTED	O. EXULTED
D. ABATED	H. KEENING	L. TENDRILS	P. STABLE

1. Withdrew; went back
2. Intense excitement
3. Twisting the face to show pain
4. Advantage; resource
5. Stuff; devour
6. Long, slender, curling strands
7. Steady; firm
8. An electronic device that sends a signal
9. Rejoiced
10. Lessened; diminished
11. Piercing; intense
12. Lifted; heaved
13. A continuous humming sound
14. Aggravating; maddening
15. Overwhelming
16. Dashed; charged

A=1	B=15	C=8	D=10
E=4	F=14	G=5	H=11
I=13	J=3	K=12	L=6
M=16	N=2	O=9	P=7

Hatchet Vocabulary Word Search 1

```
F E X A S P E R A T I O N T M W V C U Q
M L N C R C D V F Y A G T W B K H L N M
G A A C Z J G P M S C R R M N W W T W D
V R S I H S Q X V S C I A T C Y G I I M
Z R I S L S P G W H U N N X C L F N T Q
R G L M I I Y D D N R S S P C W W F T F
B Z W X A V N Z Q S A T M M S Y R U I T
R J F H V C E G R K T I I F B F D R N S
W M U Q K K I L Q S E N T V W R H I G G
R H Y N X Q M N Y X L C T G F S E A L L
E D Z R D L T H G N Y T E C U J F T Y T
N K M G G U Q N S P P I R K R M T I E Y
C Q R V F Q L E H D R V K Y O C E N X C
H J P R O N G Y G E L E N O R D D G A D
I N S Q R M P N R G E H C U H R M C B H
N R Y T E Q I W T N T J D I I L T B A B
G P U N A L F D I U B E P L O N L D T J
N O T E A G E N X L Z Y S X E U H E E K
S P R R F I G G R I S V K T X V S T D H
Q P I G M U N E R E Q Z S N E S W L Q P
W P A Y E I L E R L C I Q L A W A U S P
S T T S P P V L S I S E B V W F L X R L
J S S E M L P Z Y R N A D V S H L E X Z
L Q E M U Z V G E P T G Z E V M O K J D
P S S P C I T P E S I T N A D M W C G G
```

A continuous humming sound (5)
Advantage; resource (5)
Aggravating; maddening (11)
An electronic device that sends a signal (11)
Annoyance (12)
Correctly (10)
Dashed; charged (6)
Disinfectant; kills germs (10)
Dripping; trickling (7)
Enduring; not giving up (10)
Enormously (9)
Excessively (6)
Ground up; crumbled (10)
Intense excitement (5)
Involuntary muscle contraction (5)
Lessened; diminished (6)
Lifted; heaved (6)
Long, slender, curling strands (8)
Natural; intuitive (11)
Not knowing; not intended (11)
Overwhelming (10)
Piercing; intense (7)
Regretfully (8)

Rejoiced (7)
Roll around (6)
Rough (5)
Section; part (7)
Steady; firm (6)
Stuff; devour (5)
Stumped; stuck in puzzlement (7)
Tearing; turning; twisting (9)
Thin, pointed, projecting part (5)
Twisting the face to show pain (9)
Twisting; winding (9)
Valuable (8)
Waving or swinging vigorously (8)
Withdrew; went back (7)

Hatchet Vocabulary Word Search 1 Answer Key

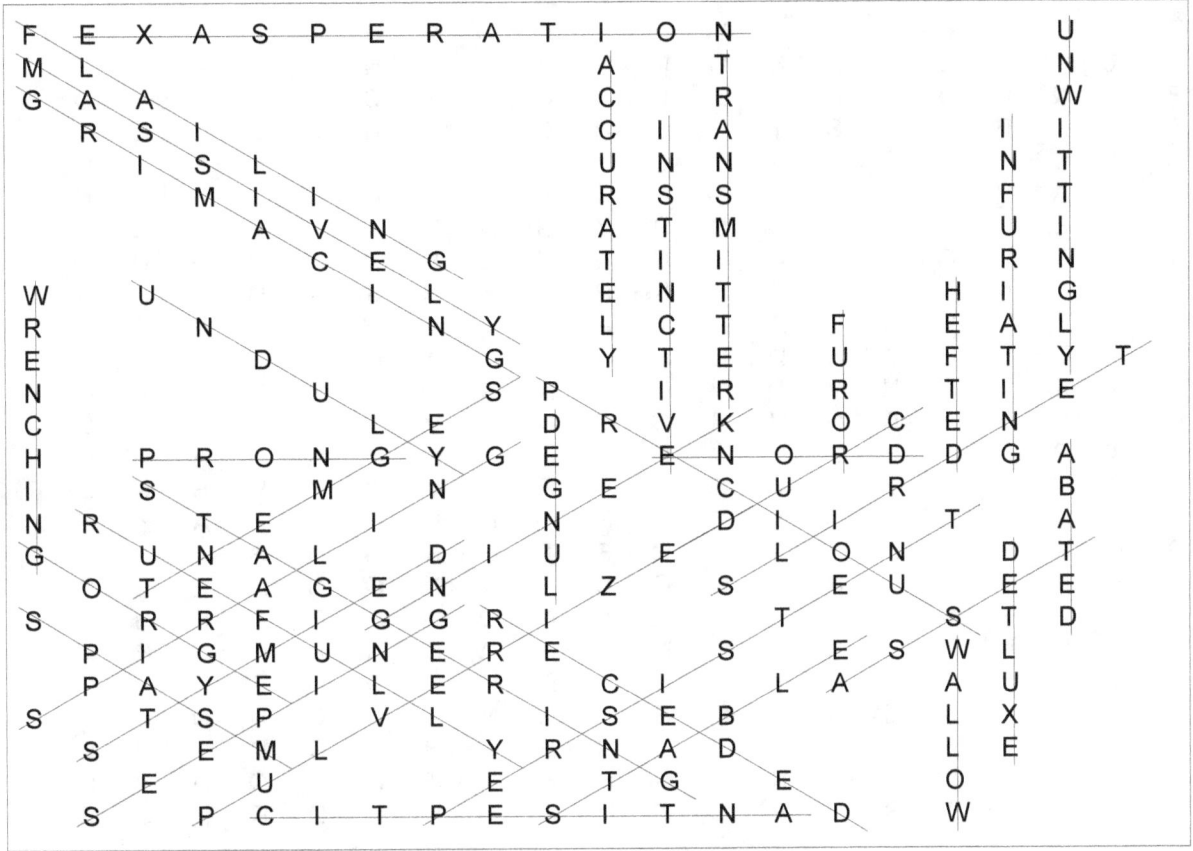

A continuous humming sound (5)
Advantage; resource (5)
Aggravating; maddening (11)
An electronic device that sends a signal (11)
Annoyance (12)
Correctly (10)
Dashed; charged (6)
Disinfectant; kills germs (10)
Dripping; trickling (7)
Enduring; not giving up (10)
Enormously (9)
Excessively (6)
Ground up; crumbled (10)
Intense excitement (5)
Involuntary muscle contraction (5)
Lessened; diminished (6)
Lifted; heaved (6)
Long, slender, curling strands (8)
Natural; intuitive (11)
Not knowing; not intended (11)
Overwhelming (10)
Piercing; intense (7)
Regretfully (8)

Rejoiced (7)
Roll around (6)
Rough (5)
Section; part (7)
Steady; firm (6)
Stuff; devour (5)
Stumped; stuck in puzzlement (7)
Tearing; turning; twisting (9)
Thin, pointed, projecting part (5)
Twisting the face to show pain (9)
Twisting; winding (9)
Valuable (8)
Waving or swinging vigorously (8)
Withdrew; went back (7)

Hatchet Vocabulary Word Search 2

```
R U E F U L L Y W A L L O W S T A B L E
G R W X D F H S Q M Y Y G B N F U M Q X
P I N F U R I A T I N G P E C S N A R D
S U K P P L S Y F J R S M N U C D S B J
C T L H E F T E D Z Y G P O T N U S Z C
R D A V W R L E T M E P I X R B L I C N
K F Z G E Y S W D S Y C B W A T Y V Q N
X J T U G R C I T F E Y L R N Z Q E H M
T R T N N E I T S R P K Y R S X D L C B
D L H W I S R Z P T P C V V M W Q Y F Y
Z Z D I L W S I E B E P P J I J G H L Y
D H X T I H V Q N D R N S Q T B B E T M
B Q S T A D N V H G Q N T V T C T N W G
G B P I L S D V M P O J J N E A N A W Q
K Q I N F T H W G I V F Z V R Z H B K J
L F R G H Y Q X T T P J I U K L H A Z H
G Y A L M M Z A X G F T C K G U S T R J
K R L Y Q I R F N G C C N N Q N J E F B
A C I T P E S I T N A N O W E G D D H B
S V N M P D H L I I P R W D N E O S R M
S R G S A C F T F P P D U I D D F R V W
E G A R N C S W C E X R N E B Q U D G C
T X H E F N I X Y E C E C H Y D R O N E
E B R C I N T N W S E E F J H F O N N P
G W S P A S M H G K R Z T E N D R I L S
```

A continuous humming sound (5)
Advantage; resource (5)
Aggravating; maddening (11)
An electronic device that sends a signal (11)
Annoyance (12)
Correctly (10)
Dashed; charged (6)
Disinfectant; kills germs (10)
Dripping; trickling (7)
Enduring; not giving up (10)
Enormously (9)
Excessively (6)
Ground up; crumbled (10)
Intense excitement (5)
Involuntary muscle contraction (5)
Lessened; diminished (6)
Lifted; heaved (6)
Long, slender, curling strands (8)
Natural; intuitive (11)
Not knowing; not intended (11)
Overwhelming (10)
Piercing; intense (7)
Regretfully (8)

Rejoiced (7)
Roll around (6)
Rough (5)
Section; part (7)
Steady; firm (6)
Stuff; devour (5)
Stumped; stuck in puzzlement (7)
Tearing; turning; twisting (9)
Thin, pointed, projecting part (5)
Twisting the face to show pain (9)
Twisting; winding (9)
Valuable (8)
Waving or swinging vigorously (8)
Withdrew; went back (7)

Hatchet Vocabulary Word Search 2 Answer Key

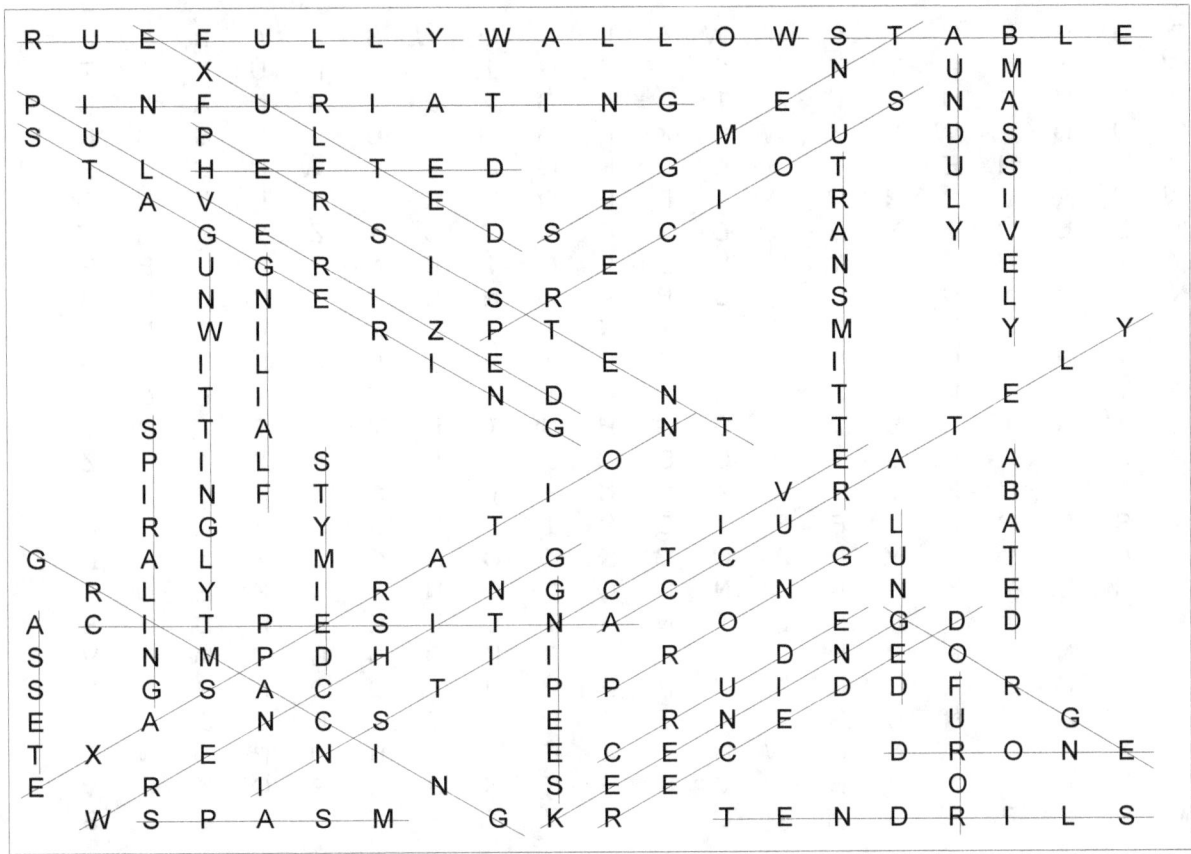

A continuous humming sound (5)
Advantage; resource (5)
Aggravating; maddening (11)
An electronic device that sends a signal (11)
Annoyance (12)
Correctly (10)
Dashed; charged (6)
Disinfectant; kills germs (10)
Dripping; trickling (7)
Enduring; not giving up (10)
Enormously (9)
Excessively (6)
Ground up; crumbled (10)
Intense excitement (5)
Involuntary muscle contraction (5)
Lessened; diminished (6)
Lifted; heaved (6)
Long, slender, curling strands (8)
Natural; intuitive (11)
Not knowing; not intended (11)
Overwhelming (10)
Piercing; intense (7)
Regretfully (8)

Rejoiced (7)
Roll around (6)
Rough (5)
Section; part (7)
Steady; firm (6)
Stuff; devour (5)
Stumped; stuck in puzzlement (7)
Tearing; turning; twisting (9)
Thin, pointed, projecting part (5)
Twisting the face to show pain (9)
Twisting; winding (9)
Valuable (8)
Waving or swinging vigorously (8)
Withdrew; went back (7)

Hatchet Vocabulary Word Search 3

R	U	E	F	U	L	L	Y	W	A	L	L	O	W	S	T	A	B	L	E
W	J	J	X	L	T	X	Z	C	J	G	G	J	V	N	F	U	M	C	T
P	I	N	F	U	R	I	A	T	I	N	G	M	E	R	S	N	A	L	D
S	U	Q	P	W	L	K	W	N	K	F	G	M	C	U	F	D	S	S	N
F	T	L	H	E	F	T	E	D	R	R	G	P	O	T	W	U	S	D	R
W	H	A	V	P	R	R	E	P	B	E	Q	I	K	R	K	L	I	N	G
K	L	L	G	E	X	S	Q	D	S	G	C	G	C	A	Z	Y	V	B	V
V	P	Z	U	G	R	Y	I	P	B	E	P	T	K	N	Z	S	E	B	F
N	K	S	N	N	E	I	D	S	R	W	Z	N	N	S	S	W	L	H	B
L	H	L	W	I	L	R	Z	P	T	K	J	Z	S	M	B	W	Y	L	Y
C	Y	B	I	L	H	L	I	E	Z	E	J	P	J	I	C	L	R	L	S
D	T	S	T	I	W	Z	X	N	D	M	N	G	D	T	K	X	E	Q	J
H	W	S	T	A	S	V	R	G	G	H	N	T	F	T	X	T	T	W	Y
H	X	P	I	L	S	T	P	C	S	O	J	K	F	E	A	X	A	L	Z
J	S	I	N	F	T	Y	K	X	I	N	H	V	V	R	X	F	B	P	F
N	S	R	G	B	Y	F	F	T	Q	S	J	I	U	G	L	F	A	L	C
G	L	A	L	L	M	H	A	Q	G	K	T	C	J	G	U	J	T	B	D
X	R	L	Y	K	I	R	Y	N	G	C	C	G	N	F	N	K	E	Q	Z
A	C	I	T	P	E	S	I	T	N	A	T	O	L	E	G	D	D	H	B
S	T	N	M	P	D	H	D	I	I	S	R	K	D	N	E	O	W	T	V
S	W	G	S	A	C	Q	T	V	P	P	V	U	I	D	D	F	R	L	F
E	W	A	K	N	C	S	Z	Y	E	P	R	N	E	Z	R	U	J	G	L
T	X	X	E	W	N	I	W	H	E	C	E	C	R	B	D	R	O	N	E
E	D	R	L	I	V	H	N	V	S	E	E	H	B	C	P	O	K	D	V
M	W	S	P	A	S	M	T	G	K	R	T	T	E	N	D	R	I	L	S

ABATED
ACCURATELY
ANTISEPTIC
ASSET
CRUDE
DRONE
EXASPERATION
EXULTED
FLAILING
FUROR
GORGE
GRIMACING
HEFTED
INFURIATING
INSTINCTIVE
KEENING
LUNGED
MASSIVELY
PERSISTENT
PRECIOUS
PRONG
PULVERIZED
RECEDED
RUEFULLY
SEEPING
SEGMENT
SPASM
SPIRALING
STABLE
STAGGERING
STYMIED
TENDRILS
TRANSMITTER
UNDULY
UNWITTINGLY
WALLOW
WRENCHING

Hatchet Vocabulary Word Search 3 Answer Key

ABATED	GORGE	PRONG	STYMIED
ACCURATELY	GRIMACING	PULVERIZED	TENDRILS
ANTISEPTIC	HEFTED	RECEDED	TRANSMITTER
ASSET	INFURIATING	RUEFULLY	UNDULY
CRUDE	INSTINCTIVE	SEEPING	UNWITTINGLY
DRONE	KEENING	SEGMENT	WALLOW
EXASPERATION	LUNGED	SPASM	WRENCHING
EXULTED	MASSIVELY	SPIRALING	
FLAILING	PERSISTENT	STABLE	
FUROR	PRECIOUS	STAGGERING	

Hatchet Vocabulary Word Search 4

```
A T R A N S M I T T E R V H M I B H A S
F C P A S D B C N J R R X S G N J G N Z
N M C N P Z Y B Z F P R Z Z R S C F T F
J H T U G I Z M L H U S D Q T Q C I T N
J L T H R S R M V W P R C M L I Q T S C
H G L B H A T A T Y L M I Z B N F K E N
C G J Q Q D T G L U M X X A Q C J L P G
M J F F B T G E E I N P P F T I G T T L
R X F N W G Q C L X N W R Y B I X Y I Z
M L L G V K J Y N Y A G I R X V N S C K
P H A H F E D K K S Q S N T S E E G D H
U Z I Z R E B Q K T S N P T T F A G H G
L Q L Q Y N X H N A H P Y E P I S F M B
V W I U H I J W J B F M P I R S N A W Y
E R N P N G P H L I X N B E A S G L S
R E G R O G N I R E G A T S S T U L V
I N P E U N E S D O F V J J I N D I K Y
Z C K C H E E D S W N T K V E N R W O M
E H H E R G F U P D A G E T U D F W Z N
D I D D M U O U E Q D L S D N E N O R D
J N G E F I D T L E Y I L E S J C O H P
Z G N D C W L E T L S H T O B P R G N K
Q T B E R U K A Y R Y M H V W U A J G Y
V V R B X B B L E Q P S R L F G L S V Y
C P D E W A K P G R I M A C I N G X M N
```

ABATED	GORGE	PRONG	STYMIED
ACCURATELY	GRIMACING	PULVERIZED	TENDRILS
ANTISEPTIC	HEFTED	RECEDED	TRANSMITTER
ASSET	INFURIATING	RUEFULLY	UNDULY
CRUDE	INSTINCTIVE	SEEPING	UNWITTINGLY
DRONE	KEENING	SEGMENT	WALLOW
EXASPERATION	LUNGED	SPASM	WRENCHING
EXULTED	MASSIVELY	SPIRALING	
FLAILING	PERSISTENT	STABLE	
FUROR	PRECIOUS	STAGGERING	

Hatchet Vocabulary Word Search 4 Answer Key

ABATED	GORGE	PRONG	STYMIED
ACCURATELY	GRIMACING	PULVERIZED	TENDRILS
ANTISEPTIC	HEFTED	RECEDED	TRANSMITTER
ASSET	INFURIATING	RUEFULLY	UNDULY
CRUDE	INSTINCTIVE	SEEPING	UNWITTINGLY
DRONE	KEENING	SEGMENT	WALLOW
EXASPERATION	LUNGED	SPASM	WRENCHING
EXULTED	MASSIVELY	SPIRALING	
FLAILING	PERSISTENT	STABLE	
FUROR	PRECIOUS	STAGGERING	

Hatchet Vocabulary Crossword 1

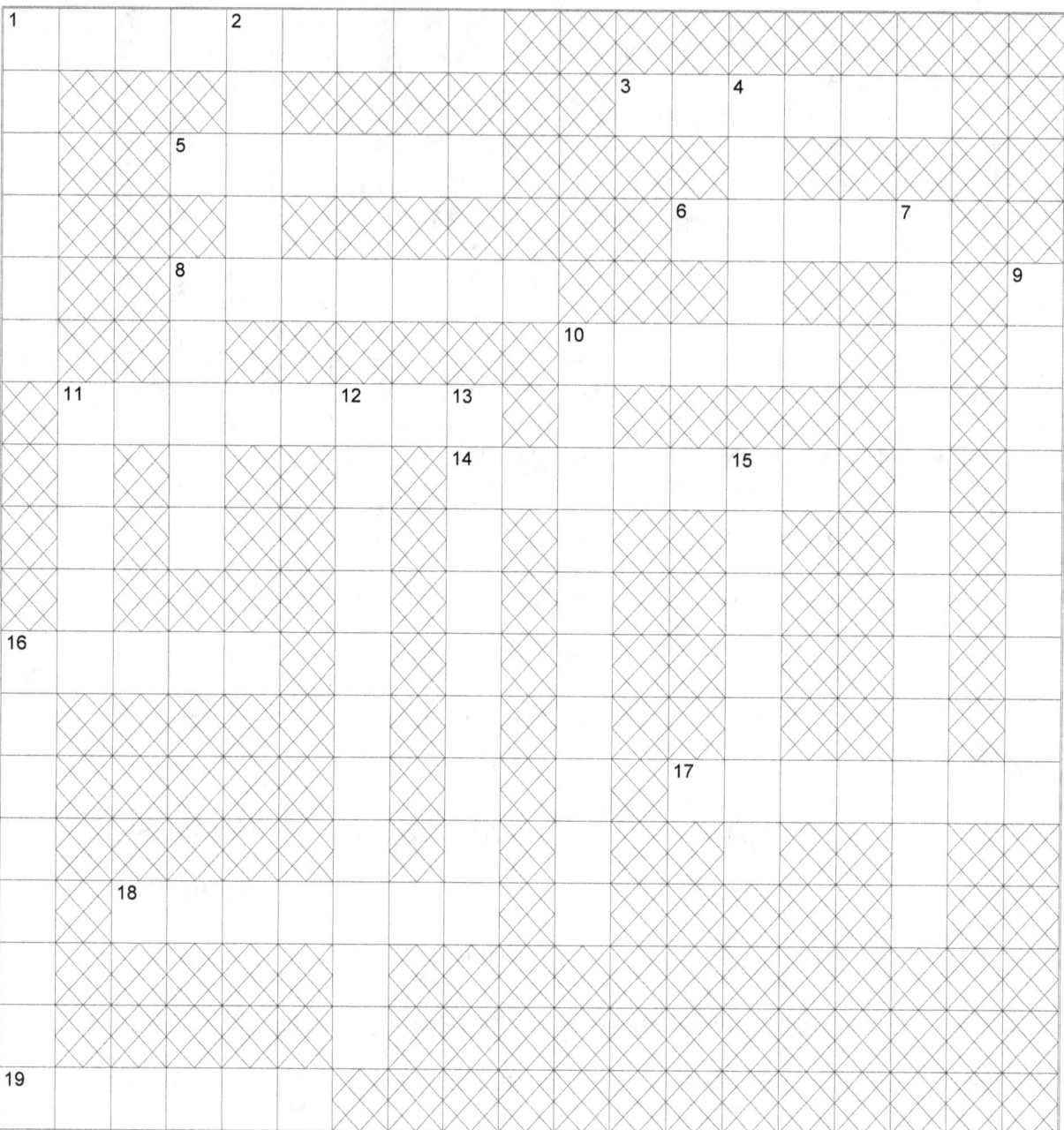

Across
1. Tearing; turning; twisting
3. Excessively
5. Dashed; charged
6. Stuff; devour
8. Section; part
10. Advantage; resource
11. Waving or swinging vigorously
14. Withdrew; went back
16. Thin, pointed, projecting part
17. Dripping; trickling
18. Piercing; intense
19. Steady; firm

Down
1. Roll around
2. Rough
4. A continuous humming sound
7. Annoyance
8. Involuntary muscle contraction
9. Twisting; winding
10. Correctly
11. Intense excitement
12. Natural; intuitive
13. Twisting the face to show pain
15. Rejoiced
16. Valuable

Hatchet Vocabulary Crossword 1 Answer Key

Across
1. Tearing; turning; twisting
3. Excessively
5. Dashed; charged
6. Stuff; devour
8. Section; part
10. Advantage; resource
11. Waving or swinging vigorously
14. Withdrew; went back
16. Thin, pointed, projecting part
17. Dripping; trickling
18. Piercing; intense
19. Steady; firm

Down
1. Roll around
2. Rough
4. A continuous humming sound
7. Annoyance
8. Involuntary muscle contraction
9. Twisting; winding
10. Correctly
11. Intense excitement
12. Natural; intuitive
13. Twisting the face to show pain
15. Rejoiced
16. Valuable

Hatchet Vocabulary Crossword 2

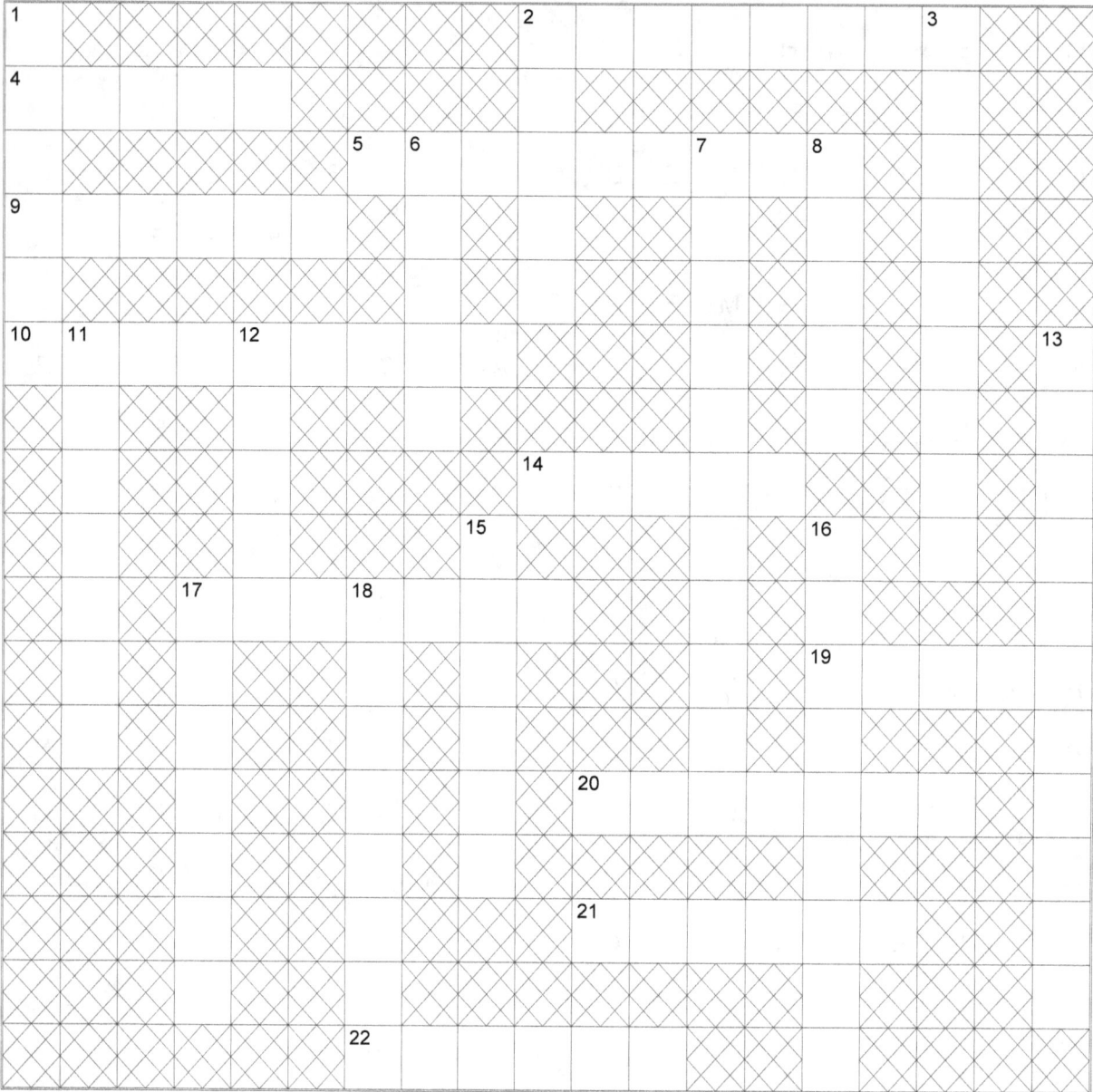

Across
2. Waving or swinging vigorously
4. Advantage; resource
5. Twisting; winding
9. Dashed; charged
10. Tearing; turning; twisting
14. A continuous humming sound
17. Dripping; trickling
19. Involuntary muscle contraction
20. Piercing; intense
21. Lifted; heaved
22. Steady; firm

Down
1. Roll around
2. Intense excitement
3. Twisting the face to show pain
6. Thin, pointed, projecting part
7. Natural; intuitive
8. Stuff; devour
11. Withdrew; went back
12. Rough
13. An electronic device that sends a signal
15. Excessively
16. Enormously
17. Section; part
18. Valuable

Hatchet Vocabulary Crossword 2 Answer Key

¹W						²F	L	A	I	L	³G	N
⁴A	S	S	E	T		U					R	
L				⁵S	⁶P	I	R	A	⁷L	⁸I	N	G
⁹L	U	N	G	E	D	R			O		M	A
O					O	R			S		A	
¹⁰W	¹¹R	E	¹²N	C	H	I	N	G		T		G	C	¹³T
	E		R		G					I		E		R
	C		U				¹⁴D	R	O	N	E		N		A
	E		D			¹⁵U			¹⁶C		M		G		N
	D		¹⁷S	¹⁸P	I	N	G		T		A				S
		D	E			D			I		¹⁹S	P	A	S	M
			G			U			V		S				I
			M			²⁰K	E	E	N	I	N	G			T
			E			Y					V				T
			N			²¹H	E	F	T	E	D				E
			T			U					L				R
				²²S	T	A	B	L	E		Y				

Across
2. Waving or swinging vigorously
4. Advantage; resource
5. Twisting; winding
9. Dashed; charged
10. Tearing; turning; twisting
14. A continuous humming sound
17. Dripping; trickling
19. Involuntary muscle contraction
20. Piercing; intense
21. Lifted; heaved
22. Steady; firm

Down
1. Roll around
2. Intense excitement
3. Twisting the face to show pain
6. Thin, pointed, projecting part
7. Natural; intuitive
8. Stuff; devour
11. Withdrew; went back
12. Rough
13. An electronic device that sends a signal
15. Excessively
16. Enormously
17. Section; part
18. Valuable

Hatchet Vocabulary Crossword 3

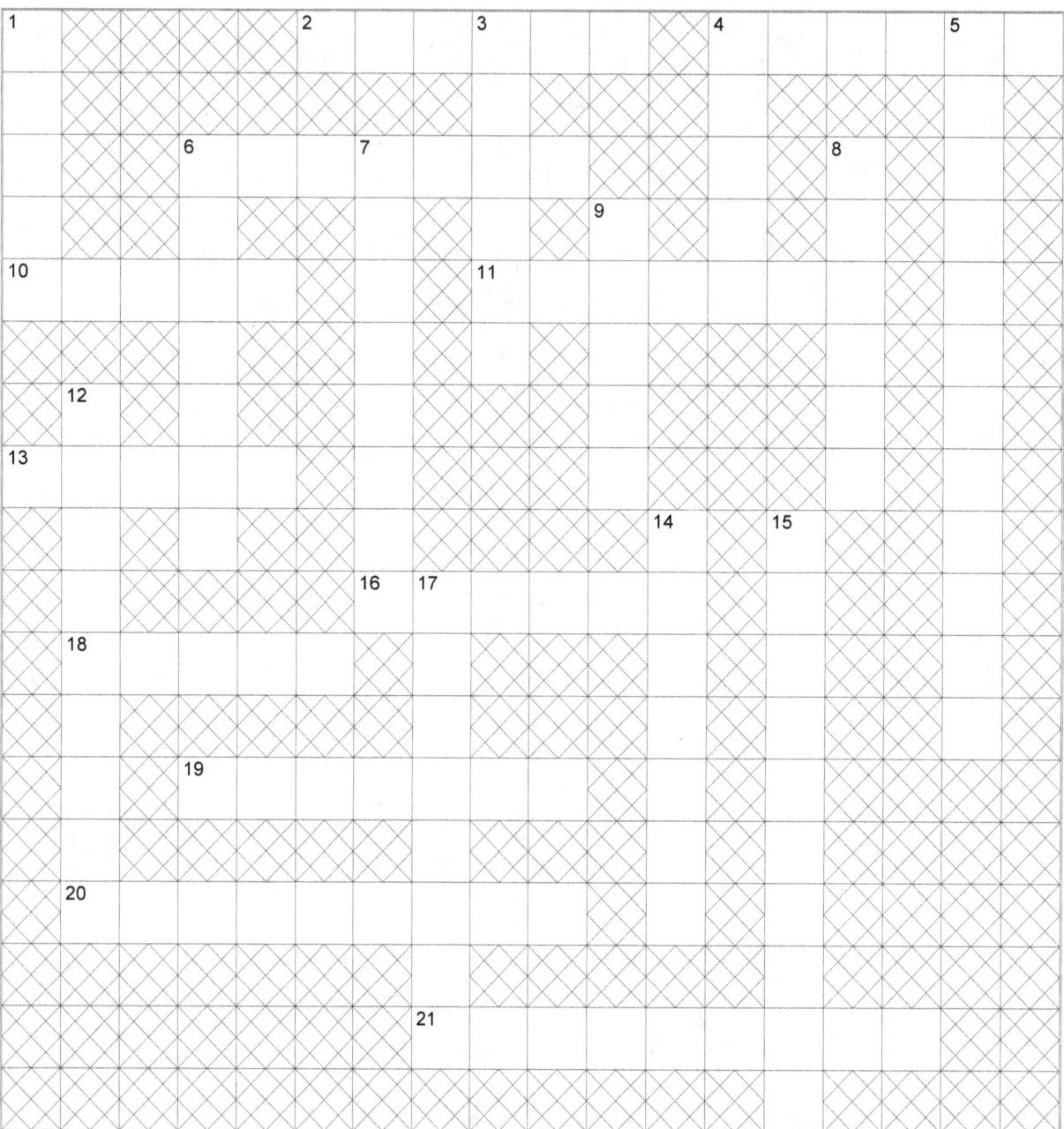

Across
2. Roll around
4. Lessened; diminished
6. Dripping; trickling
10. Stuff; devour
11. Rejoiced
13. A continuous humming sound
16. Steady; firm
18. Rough
19. Withdrew; went back
20. Twisting the face to show pain
21. Twisting; winding

Down
1. Thin, pointed, projecting part
3. Dashed; charged
4. Advantage; resource
5. Annoyance
6. Section; part
7. Valuable
8. Excessively
9. Intense excitement
12. Tearing; turning; twisting
14. Piercing; intense
15. Disinfectant; kills germs
17. Long, slender, curling strands

Hatchet Vocabulary Crossword 3 Answer Key

	1 P		2 W	A	L	3 L	O	W	4 A	B	A	T	5 E	D
	R					U			S				X	
	O		6 S	E	7 P	I	N	G	S		8 U		A	
	N		E		R		G	9 F	E		N		S	
10 G	O	R	G	E		11 E	X	U	L	T	E	D	P	
			M		C		D	R			U		E	
	12 W		E		I			O			L		R	
13 D	R	O	N	E				R			Y		A	
	E		T						14 K	15 A			T	
	N				16 S	17 T	A	B	L	E			I	
	18 C	R	U	D	E		E		E		T		O	
	H						N		N		I		N	
	I		19 R	E	C	E	D	E	D		S			
	N						R		I		E			
	20 G	R	I	M	A	C	I	N	G		P			
							L				T			
					21 S	P	I	R	A	L	I	N	G	
											C			

Across
2. Roll around
4. Lessened; diminished
6. Dripping; trickling
10. Stuff; devour
11. Rejoiced
13. A continuous humming sound
16. Steady; firm
18. Rough
19. Withdrew; went back
20. Twisting the face to show pain
21. Twisting; winding

Down
1. Thin, pointed, projecting part
3. Dashed; charged
4. Advantage; resource
5. Annoyance
6. Section; part
7. Valuable
8. Excessively
9. Intense excitement
12. Tearing; turning; twisting
14. Piercing; intense
15. Disinfectant; kills germs
17. Long, slender, curling strands

Hatchet Vocabulary Crossword 4

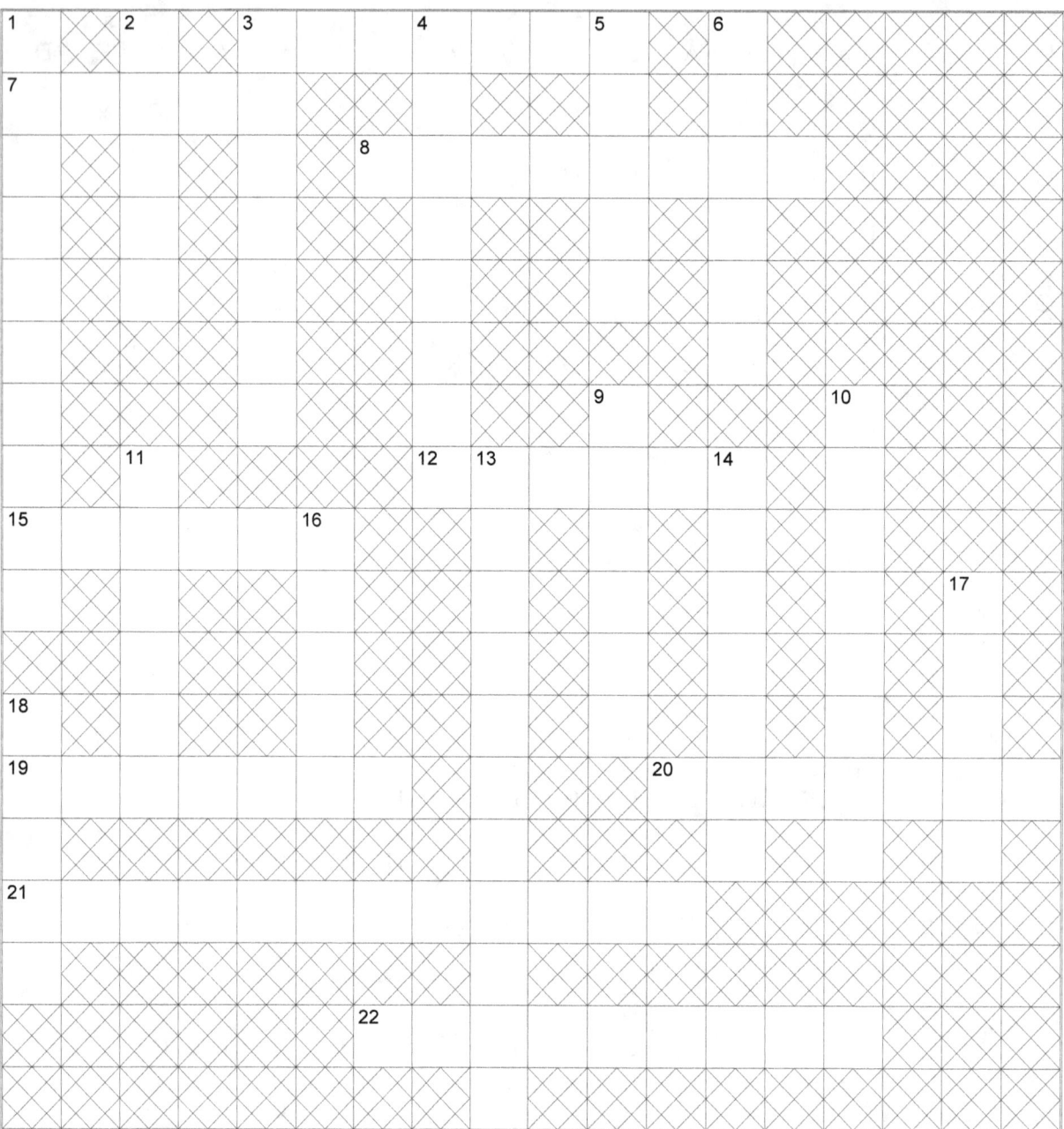

Across
3. Dripping; trickling
7. Rough
8. Long, slender, curling strands
12. Steady; firm
15. Dashed; charged
19. Stumped; stuck in puzzlement
20. Piercing; intense
21. Annoyance
22. Tearing; turning; twisting

Down
1. Correctly
2. Intense excitement
3. Section; part
4. Valuable
5. Stuff; devour
6. Roll around
9. Lessened; diminished
10. Waving or swinging vigorously
11. Excessively
13. An electronic device that sends a signal
14. Rejoiced
16. A continuous humming sound
17. Thin, pointed, projecting part
18. Advantage; resource

Hatchet Vocabulary Crossword 4 Answer Key

	1 A		2 F		3 S	E	E	4 P	I	N	5 G		6 W	
7	C	R	U	D	E			R			O		A	
	C		R		G		8 T	E	N	D	R	I	L	S
	U		O		M			C			G		L	
	R		R		E			I			E		O	
	A		N					O					W	
	T							U		9 A		10 F		
	E		11 U			12 S	13 T	A	B	L	14 E			
15 L	U	N	G	E	16 D		R		A		X		A	
Y			D		R		A		T		U		I	17 P
			U		O		N		E		L		L	R
18 A			L		N		S		D		T		I	O
19 S	T	Y	M	I	E	D		M			20 K	E	E	N	I	N	G
S								I			D		G		G
21 E	X	A	S	P	E	R	A	T	I	O	N			
T								T						
					22 W	R	E	N	C	H	I	N	G	
								R						

Across
- 3. Dripping; trickling
- 7. Rough
- 8. Long, slender, curling strands
- 12. Steady; firm
- 15. Dashed; charged
- 19. Stumped; stuck in puzzlement
- 20. Piercing; intense
- 21. Annoyance
- 22. Tearing; turning; twisting

Down
- 1. Correctly
- 2. Intense excitement
- 3. Section; part
- 4. Valuable
- 5. Stuff; devour
- 6. Roll around
- 9. Lessened; diminished
- 10. Waving or swinging vigorously
- 11. Excessively
- 13. An electronic device that sends a signal
- 14. Rejoiced
- 16. A continuous humming sound
- 17. Thin, pointed, projecting part
- 18. Advantage; resource

Hatchet Vocabulary Juggle Letters 1

1. RVZLPDEIEU = 1. _____
   Ground up; crumbled

2. EISTSPETRN = 2. _____
   Enduring; not giving up

3. IRCINMGGA = 3. _____
   Twisting the face to show pain

4. ETLABS = 4. _____
   Steady; firm

5. EUCOSIPR = 5. _____
   Valuable

6. INSMTTARETR = 6. _____
   An electronic device that sends a signal

7. EYITDSM = 7. _____
   Stumped; stuck in puzzlement

8. SIEVALMYS = 8. _____
   Enormously

9. GPRON = 9. _____
   Thin, pointed, projecting part

10. TAAEDB =10. _____
    Lessened; diminished

11. WLWALO =11. _____
    Roll around

12. LRDTESIN =12. _____
    Long, slender, curling strands

13. NFILGAIL =13. _____
    Waving or swinging vigorously

14. IENKENG =14. _____
    Piercing; intense

15. EDUCR =15. _____
    Rough

Hatchet Vocabulary Juggle Letters 1 Answer Key

1. RVZLPDEIEU = 1. PULVERIZED
   Ground up; crumbled

2. EISTSPETRN = 2. PERSISTENT
   Enduring; not giving up

3. IRCINMGGA = 3. GRIMACING
   Twisting the face to show pain

4. ETLABS = 4. STABLE
   Steady; firm

5. EUCOSIPR = 5. PRECIOUS
   Valuable

6. INSMTTARETR = 6. TRANSMITTER
   An electronic device that sends a signal

7. EYITDSM = 7. STYMIED
   Stumped; stuck in puzzlement

8. SIEVALMYS = 8. MASSIVELY
   Enormously

9. GPRON = 9. PRONG
   Thin, pointed, projecting part

10. TAAEDB =10. ABATED
    Lessened; diminished

11. WLWALO =11. WALLOW
    Roll around

12. LRDTESIN =12. TENDRILS
    Long, slender, curling strands

13. NFILGAIL =13. FLAILING
    Waving or swinging vigorously

14. IENKENG =14. KEENING
    Piercing; intense

15. EDUCR =15. CRUDE
    Rough

Hatchet Vocabulary Juggle Letters 2

1. NITSLDER = 1. _____
   Long, slender, curling strands

2. EYRLUFUL = 2. _____
   Regretfully

3. NLWITGYNITU = 3. _____
   Not knowing; not intended

4. EASTS = 4. _____
   Advantage; resource

5. SBATEL = 5. _____
   Steady; firm

6. OENDR = 6. _____
   A continuous humming sound

7. EHTEDF = 7. _____
   Lifted; heaved

8. OALLWW = 8. _____
   Roll around

9. EGMNSTE = 9. _____
   Section; part

10. PINASETITC = 10. _____
    Disinfectant; kills germs

11. DGLNUE = 11. _____
    Dashed; charged

12. RNHIEWCNG = 12. _____
    Tearing; turning; twisting

13. TTSTIRANEMR = 13. _____
    An electronic device that sends a signal

14. DDEEECR = 14. _____
    Withdrew; went back

15. IASINPRLG = 15. _____
    Twisting; winding

Hatchet Vocabulary Jugle Letters 2 Answer Key

1. NITSLDER = 1. TENDRILS
Long, slender, curling strands

2. EYRLUFUL = 2. RUEFULLY
Regretfully

3. NLWITGYNITU = 3. UNWITTINGLY
Not knowing; not intended

4. EASTS = 4. ASSET
Advantage; resource

5. SBATEL = 5. STABLE
Steady; firm

6. OENDR = 6. DRONE
A continuous humming sound

7. EHTEDF = 7. HEFTED
Lifted; heaved

8. OALLWW = 8. WALLOW
Roll around

9. EGMNSTE = 9. SEGMENT
Section; part

10. PINASETITC =10. ANTISEPTIC
Disinfectant; kills germs

11. DGLNUE =11. LUNGED
Dashed; charged

12. RNHIEWCNG =12. WRENCHING
Tearing; turning; twisting

13. TTSTIRANEMR =13. TRANSMITTER
An electronic device that sends a signal

14. DDEEECR =14. RECEDED
Withdrew; went back

15. IASINPRLG =15. SPIRALING
Twisting; winding

Hatchet Vocabulary Juggle Letters 3

1. EEHTDF = 1. _____
   Lifted; heaved

2. RRSTNITMTAE = 2. _____
   An electronic device that sends a signal

3. TNSEEMG = 3. _____
   Section; part

4. BLTESA = 4. _____
   Steady; firm

5. NSEETPRTIS = 5. _____
   Enduring; not giving up

6. DETMYSI = 6. _____
   Stumped; stuck in puzzlement

7. NNTAGIRIIFU = 7. _____
   Aggravating; maddening

8. LNUIYTWIGTN = 8. _____
   Not knowing; not intended

9. IATNPETISC = 9. _____
   Disinfectant; kills germs

10. NNCWREGIH =10. _____
    Tearing; turning; twisting

11. GIAESGGTRN =11. _____
    Overwhelming

12. ESLMAYVIS =12. _____
    Enormously

13. ASSET =13. _____
    Advantage; resource

14. URECD =14. _____
    Rough

15. GEESPIN =15. _____
    Dripping; trickling

Hatchet Vocabulary Juggle Letters 3 Answer Key

1. EEHTDF = 1. HEFTED
   Lifted; heaved

2. RRSTNITMTAE = 2. TRANSMITTER
   An electronic device that sends a signal

3. TNSEEMG = 3. SEGMENT
   Section; part

4. BLTESA = 4. STABLE
   Steady; firm

5. NSEETPRTIS = 5. PERSISTENT
   Enduring; not giving up

6. DETMYSI = 6. STYMIED
   Stumped; stuck in puzzlement

7. NNTAGIRIIFU = 7. INFURIATING
   Aggravating; maddening

8. LNUIYTWIGTN = 8. UNWITTINGLY
   Not knowing; not intended

9. IATNPETISC = 9. ANTISEPTIC
   Disinfectant; kills germs

10. NNCWREGIH = 10. WRENCHING
    Tearing; turning; twisting

11. GIAESGGTRN = 11. STAGGERING
    Overwhelming

12. ESLMAYVIS = 12. MASSIVELY
    Enormously

13. ASSET = 13. ASSET
    Advantage; resource

14. URECD = 14. CRUDE
    Rough

15. GEESPIN = 15. SEEPING
    Dripping; trickling

Hatchet Vocabulary Juggle Letters 4

1. RGGEO = 1. _____
   Stuff; devour

2. PSERANIOATXE = 2. _____
   Annoyance

3. DNGULE = 3. _____
   Dashed; charged

4. LETEXDU = 4. _____
   Rejoiced

5. UAEACCLTRY = 5. _____
   Correctly

6. FGINANRIIUT = 6. _____
   Aggravating; maddening

7. YGITNLWUNTI = 7. _____
   Not knowing; not intended

8. CAIGNGRIM = 8. _____
   Twisting the face to show pain

9. TMTRTEINSAR = 9. _____
   An electronic device that sends a signal

10. RIPESTSTNE =10. _____
    Enduring; not giving up

11. STASE =11. _____
    Advantage; resource

12. YSESAIMLV =12. _____
    Enormously

13. LTBEAS =13. _____
    Steady; firm

14. NDUUYL =14. _____
    Excessively

15. INNCWERGH =15. _____
    Tearing; turning; twisting

Hatchet Vocabulary Juggle Letters 4 Answer Key

1. RGGEO = 1. GORGE
Stuff; devour

2. PSERANIOATXE = 2. EXASPERATION
Annoyance

3. DNGULE = 3. LUNGED
Dashed; charged

4. LETEXDU = 4. EXULTED
Rejoiced

5. UAEACCLTRY = 5. ACCURATELY
Correctly

6. FGINANRIIUT = 6. INFURIATING
Aggravating; maddening

7. YGITNLWUNTI = 7. UNWITTINGLY
Not knowing; not intended

8. CAIGNGRIM = 8. GRIMACING
Twisting the face to show pain

9. TMTRTEINSAR = 9. TRANSMITTER
An electronic device that sends a signal

10. RIPESTSTNE =10. PERSISTENT
Enduring; not giving up

11. STASE =11. ASSET
Advantage; resource

12. YSESAIMLV =12. MASSIVELY
Enormously

13. LTBEAS =13. STABLE
Steady; firm

14. NDUUYL =14. UNDULY
Excessively

15. INNCWERGH =15. WRENCHING
Tearing; turning; twisting

ABATED	Lessened; diminished
ACCURATELY	Correctly
ANTISEPTIC	Disinfectant; kills germs
ASSET	Advantage; resource
CRUDE	Rough
DRONE	A continuous humming sound

EXASPERATION	Annoyance
EXULTED	Rejoiced
FLAILING	Waving or swinging vigorously
FUROR	Intense excitement
GORGE	Stuff; devour
GRIMACING	Twisting the face to show pain

HEFTED	Lifted; heaved
INFURIATING	Aggravating; maddening
INSTINCTIVE	Natural; intuitive
KEENING	Piercing; intense
LUNGED	Dashed; charged
MASSIVELY	Enormously

PERSISTENT	Enduring; not giving up
PRECIOUS	Valuable
PRONG	Thin, pointed, projecting part
PULVERIZED	Ground up; crumbled
RECEDED	Withdrew; went back
RUEFULLY	Regretfully

SEEPING	Dripping; trickling
SEGMENT	Section; part
SPASM	Involuntary muscle contraction
SPIRALING	Twisting; winding
STABLE	Steady; firm
STAGGERING	Overwhelming

STYMIED	Stumped; stuck in puzzlement
TENDRILS	Long, slender, curling strands
TRANSMITTER	An electronic device that sends a signal
UNDULY	Excessively
UNWITTINGLY	Not knowing; not intended
WALLOW	Roll around

WRENCHING	Tearing; turning; twisting

Hatchet Vocabulary

UNWITTINGLY	EXASPERATION	LUNGED	SEGMENT	PULVERIZED
UNDULY	SPIRALING	KEENING	PERSISTENT	INSTINCTIVE
GRIMACING	FLAILING	FREE SPACE	STABLE	STYMIED
MASSIVELY	TRANSMITTER	STAGGERING	SPASM	TENDRILS
PRONG	ABATED	PRECIOUS	INFURIATING	RUEFULLY

Hatchet Vocabulary

HEFTED	WALLOW	ASSET	ACCURATELY	DRONE
ANTISEPTIC	SEEPING	RECEDED	FUROR	CRUDE
EXULTED	WRENCHING	FREE SPACE	INFURIATING	PRECIOUS
ABATED	PRONG	TENDRILS	SPASM	STAGGERING
TRANSMITTER	MASSIVELY	STYMIED	STABLE	GORGE

Hatchet Vocabulary

GORGE	INSTINCTIVE	SPIRALING	PULVERIZED	MASSIVELY
STYMIED	TENDRILS	HEFTED	FUROR	STABLE
PRECIOUS	GRIMACING	FREE SPACE	UNDULY	FLAILING
RECEDED	INFURIATING	CRUDE	LUNGED	ACCURATELY
PRONG	TRANSMITTER	WALLOW	EXASPERATION	SEGMENT

Hatchet Vocabulary

SEEPING	EXULTED	DRONE	STAGGERING	SPASM
UNWITTINGLY	KEENING	ABATED	WRENCHING	ANTISEPTIC
ASSET	PERSISTENT	FREE SPACE	EXASPERATION	WALLOW
TRANSMITTER	PRONG	ACCURATELY	LUNGED	CRUDE
INFURIATING	RECEDED	FLAILING	UNDULY	RUEFULLY

Hatchet Vocabulary

EXULTED	LUNGED	ACCURATELY	UNDULY	STABLE
SPIRALING	ANTISEPTIC	HEFTED	ASSET	INFURIATING
GORGE	UNWITTINGLY	FREE SPACE	GRIMACING	RUEFULLY
SEEPING	PRECIOUS	MASSIVELY	KEENING	EXASPERATION
PULVERIZED	SPASM	PERSISTENT	TENDRILS	SEGMENT

Hatchet Vocabulary

PRONG	DRONE	STAGGERING	CRUDE	FUROR
INSTINCTIVE	TRANSMITTER	FLAILING	WALLOW	STYMIED
ABATED	WRENCHING	FREE SPACE	TENDRILS	PERSISTENT
SPASM	PULVERIZED	EXASPERATION	KEENING	MASSIVELY
PRECIOUS	SEEPING	RUEFULLY	GRIMACING	RECEDED

Hatchet Vocabulary

INFURIATING	RUEFULLY	INSTINCTIVE	FLAILING	WALLOW
PRECIOUS	SPASM	EXULTED	SPIRALING	SEGMENT
CRUDE	STYMIED	FREE SPACE	WRENCHING	TRANSMITTER
LUNGED	PRONG	GORGE	STABLE	KEENING
GRIMACING	TENDRILS	RECEDED	PERSISTENT	UNWITTINGLY

Hatchet Vocabulary

PULVERIZED	FUROR	HEFTED	UNDULY	ACCURATELY
ABATED	ANTISEPTIC	STAGGERING	MASSIVELY	EXASPERATION
SEEPING	ASSET	FREE SPACE	PERSISTENT	RECEDED
TENDRILS	GRIMACING	KEENING	STABLE	GORGE
PRONG	LUNGED	TRANSMITTER	WRENCHING	DRONE

Hatchet Vocabulary

FLAILING	UNDULY	MASSIVELY	INSTINCTIVE	DRONE
PULVERIZED	GORGE	PRONG	SEEPING	KEENING
EXULTED	FUROR	FREE SPACE	INFURIATING	TRANSMITTER
EXASPERATION	HEFTED	SPIRALING	CRUDE	WALLOW
UNWITTINGLY	PERSISTENT	LUNGED	ASSET	STABLE

Hatchet Vocabulary

GRIMACING	ABATED	RECEDED	SPASM	RUEFULLY
WRENCHING	PRECIOUS	STAGGERING	SEGMENT	ACCURATELY
TENDRILS	ANTISEPTIC	FREE SPACE	ASSET	LUNGED
PERSISTENT	UNWITTINGLY	WALLOW	CRUDE	SPIRALING
HEFTED	EXASPERATION	TRANSMITTER	INFURIATING	STYMIED

Hatchet Vocabulary

INFURIATING	UNWITTINGLY	STAGGERING	INSTINCTIVE	DRONE
TRANSMITTER	WALLOW	CRUDE	KEENING	PRONG
ABATED	GORGE	FREE SPACE	RUEFULLY	LUNGED
MASSIVELY	FUROR	SEEPING	EXULTED	STABLE
FLAILING	GRIMACING	ASSET	PERSISTENT	SPASM

Hatchet Vocabulary

ACCURATELY	EXASPERATION	STYMIED	UNDULY	RECEDED
PULVERIZED	SEGMENT	WRENCHING	PRECIOUS	HEFTED
SPIRALING	TENDRILS	FREE SPACE	PERSISTENT	ASSET
GRIMACING	FLAILING	STABLE	EXULTED	SEEPING
FUROR	MASSIVELY	LUNGED	RUEFULLY	ANTISEPTIC

Hatchet Vocabulary

LUNGED	UNDULY	STAGGERING	STABLE	WALLOW
KEENING	ANTISEPTIC	INSTINCTIVE	TRANSMITTER	EXASPERATION
ASSET	CRUDE	FREE SPACE	DRONE	GRIMACING
SEEPING	MASSIVELY	SPASM	ACCURATELY	SPIRALING
EXULTED	STYMIED	INFURIATING	SEGMENT	PRONG

Hatchet Vocabulary

FUROR	FLAILING	HEFTED	PERSISTENT	RUEFULLY
RECEDED	TENDRILS	GORGE	UNWITTINGLY	ABATED
PULVERIZED	WRENCHING	FREE SPACE	SEGMENT	INFURIATING
STYMIED	EXULTED	SPIRALING	ACCURATELY	SPASM
MASSIVELY	SEEPING	GRIMACING	DRONE	PRECIOUS

Hatchet Vocabulary

KEENING	SPIRALING	INFURIATING	INSTINCTIVE	RECEDED
ASSET	FLAILING	SPASM	HEFTED	STABLE
FUROR	MASSIVELY	FREE SPACE	ANTISEPTIC	PULVERIZED
RUEFULLY	SEEPING	TENDRILS	STAGGERING	WALLOW
GORGE	PRONG	SEGMENT	WRENCHING	CRUDE

Hatchet Vocabulary

PERSISTENT	STYMIED	GRIMACING	UNDULY	PRECIOUS
TRANSMITTER	EXASPERATION	LUNGED	UNWITTINGLY	ACCURATELY
EXULTED	ABATED	FREE SPACE	WRENCHING	SEGMENT
PRONG	GORGE	WALLOW	STAGGERING	TENDRILS
SEEPING	RUEFULLY	PULVERIZED	ANTISEPTIC	DRONE

Hatchet Vocabulary

RECEDED	UNWITTINGLY	PRONG	SEEPING	FLAILING
PULVERIZED	MASSIVELY	HEFTED	STAGGERING	STYMIED
ACCURATELY	GORGE	FREE SPACE	TRANSMITTER	KEENING
ABATED	INSTINCTIVE	WRENCHING	SPIRALING	RUEFULLY
TENDRILS	STABLE	ASSET	DRONE	PERSISTENT

Hatchet Vocabulary

INFURIATING	LUNGED	UNDULY	WALLOW	SPASM
PRECIOUS	ANTISEPTIC	EXASPERATION	CRUDE	GRIMACING
EXULTED	SEGMENT	FREE SPACE	DRONE	ASSET
STABLE	TENDRILS	RUEFULLY	SPIRALING	WRENCHING
INSTINCTIVE	ABATED	KEENING	TRANSMITTER	FUROR

Hatchet Vocabulary

FLAILING	PULVERIZED	INSTINCTIVE	WRENCHING	ACCURATELY
WALLOW	STABLE	UNWITTINGLY	ABATED	KEENING
SPASM	SEGMENT	FREE SPACE	PRONG	MASSIVELY
PERSISTENT	PRECIOUS	EXULTED	SEEPING	UNDULY
TRANSMITTER	SPIRALING	RUEFULLY	ASSET	RECEDED

Hatchet Vocabulary

HEFTED	CRUDE	LUNGED	DRONE	FUROR
TENDRILS	ANTISEPTIC	EXASPERATION	GORGE	GRIMACING
STYMIED	INFURIATING	FREE SPACE	ASSET	RUEFULLY
SPIRALING	TRANSMITTER	UNDULY	SEEPING	EXULTED
PRECIOUS	PERSISTENT	MASSIVELY	PRONG	STAGGERING

Hatchet Vocabulary

MASSIVELY	PRECIOUS	PERSISTENT	TRANSMITTER	SEGMENT
KEENING	WRENCHING	STYMIED	FUROR	RECEDED
EXASPERATION	ACCURATELY	FREE SPACE	UNDULY	LUNGED
CRUDE	EXULTED	SPASM	RUEFULLY	FLAILING
SEEPING	STAGGERING	ABATED	TENDRILS	ASSET

Hatchet Vocabulary

ANTISEPTIC	GRIMACING	DRONE	STABLE	UNWITTINGLY
INSTINCTIVE	INFURIATING	PULVERIZED	SPIRALING	PRONG
GORGE	HEFTED	FREE SPACE	TENDRILS	ABATED
STAGGERING	SEEPING	FLAILING	RUEFULLY	SPASM
EXULTED	CRUDE	LUNGED	UNDULY	WALLOW

Hatchet Vocabulary

UNWITTINGLY	ASSET	SPASM	FUROR	FLAILING
UNDULY	CRUDE	LUNGED	PERSISTENT	RECEDED
ABATED	TRANSMITTER	FREE SPACE	PRECIOUS	ACCURATELY
KEENING	PRONG	RUEFULLY	EXASPERATION	GRIMACING
TENDRILS	SEEPING	GORGE	INFURIATING	EXULTED

Hatchet Vocabulary

STYMIED	HEFTED	PULVERIZED	MASSIVELY	STAGGERING
WALLOW	SEGMENT	SPIRALING	INSTINCTIVE	ANTISEPTIC
STABLE	WRENCHING	FREE SPACE	INFURIATING	GORGE
SEEPING	TENDRILS	GRIMACING	EXASPERATION	RUEFULLY
PRONG	KEENING	ACCURATELY	PRECIOUS	DRONE

Hatchet Vocabulary

WRENCHING	KEENING	PRONG	MASSIVELY	EXULTED
SPASM	GORGE	PULVERIZED	WALLOW	PERSISTENT
FUROR	DRONE	FREE SPACE	CRUDE	RUEFULLY
SPIRALING	INSTINCTIVE	RECEDED	INFURIATING	STAGGERING
EXASPERATION	ASSET	TENDRILS	FLAILING	UNDULY

Hatchet Vocabulary

LUNGED	ANTISEPTIC	SEGMENT	STYMIED	HEFTED
ACCURATELY	UNWITTINGLY	TRANSMITTER	STABLE	GRIMACING
ABATED	PRECIOUS	FREE SPACE	FLAILING	TENDRILS
ASSET	EXASPERATION	STAGGERING	INFURIATING	RECEDED
INSTINCTIVE	SPIRALING	RUEFULLY	CRUDE	SEEPING

Hatchet Vocabulary

HEFTED	GRIMACING	EXASPERATION	EXULTED	PRECIOUS
PRONG	WALLOW	DRONE	SEEPING	ABATED
KEENING	SEGMENT	FREE SPACE	LUNGED	UNWITTINGLY
UNDULY	SPIRALING	STABLE	WRENCHING	RUEFULLY
MASSIVELY	ASSET	ANTISEPTIC	INSTINCTIVE	ACCURATELY

Hatchet Vocabulary

CRUDE	GORGE	INFURIATING	FLAILING	FUROR
PERSISTENT	SPASM	TRANSMITTER	STAGGERING	RECEDED
PULVERIZED	TENDRILS	FREE SPACE	INSTINCTIVE	ANTISEPTIC
ASSET	MASSIVELY	RUEFULLY	WRENCHING	STABLE
SPIRALING	UNDULY	UNWITTINGLY	LUNGED	STYMIED

Hatchet Vocabulary

PRECIOUS	PULVERIZED	SPIRALING	WALLOW	SEGMENT
KEENING	ABATED	GORGE	ASSET	STAGGERING
WRENCHING	ANTISEPTIC	FREE SPACE	INFURIATING	EXASPERATION
UNWITTINGLY	HEFTED	DRONE	RECEDED	FLAILING
SEEPING	MASSIVELY	STYMIED	PERSISTENT	SPASM

Hatchet Vocabulary

ACCURATELY	TENDRILS	EXULTED	LUNGED	PRONG
FUROR	STABLE	CRUDE	TRANSMITTER	RUEFULLY
GRIMACING	INSTINCTIVE	FREE SPACE	PERSISTENT	STYMIED
MASSIVELY	SEEPING	FLAILING	RECEDED	DRONE
HEFTED	UNWITTINGLY	EXASPERATION	INFURIATING	UNDULY

Hatchet Vocabulary

HEFTED	STAGGERING	PRECIOUS	MASSIVELY	WRENCHING
SPIRALING	SPASM	DRONE	PRONG	PULVERIZED
GORGE	GRIMACING	FREE SPACE	INSTINCTIVE	EXULTED
UNWITTINGLY	SEEPING	ASSET	STYMIED	EXASPERATION
ANTISEPTIC	LUNGED	CRUDE	INFURIATING	TENDRILS

Hatchet Vocabulary

FLAILING	WALLOW	RUEFULLY	RECEDED	UNDULY
FUROR	KEENING	ABATED	SEGMENT	PERSISTENT
ACCURATELY	TRANSMITTER	FREE SPACE	INFURIATING	CRUDE
LUNGED	ANTISEPTIC	EXASPERATION	STYMIED	ASSET
SEEPING	UNWITTINGLY	EXULTED	INSTINCTIVE	STABLE

www.ingramcontent.com/pod-product-compliance
Lightning Source LLC
Chambersburg PA
CBHW081456070526
44586CB00019B/2388